Short-Term Missions

A Christian Guide To STMs

For Leaders, Pastors, Churches, Students, STM Teams
And Mission Organizations – Survive And Thrive!

Mathew Backholer

Short-Term Missions, A Christian Guide to STMs
For Leaders, Pastors, Churches, Students, STM Teams and Mission
Organizations – Survive and Thrive!

ISBN 978-1-907066-49-8 (paperback)
ISBN 978-1-907066-50-4 (eBook ePub)
British Library Cataloguing In Publication Data
A Record of this Publication is available from the British Library
First Published in May 2016 by ByFaith Media. Revised and
updated in August 2017 – www.MissionsNow.co.uk.

- Jesus Christ is Lord -

Contents

Jesus said, "Go into all the world and preach the gospel to every creature. He who believes and is baptised will be saved; but he who does not believe will be condemned" (Mark 16:15-16).

'As cold water to a weary soul, so is good news from a far country' (Proverbs 25:25).

Jesus said, "And other sheep I have which are not of this fold; them also I must bring, and they will hear My voice; and there will be one flock and one shepherd" (John 10:16).

Jesus said, "Go therefore and make disciples of all the nations …teaching them to observe all things that I have commanded you; and lo, I am with you always, even to the end of the age" (Matthew 28:19-20).

Preface

'To him who knows to do good and does not do it, to him it is sin' (James 4:17).

The author has been on more than thirty short-term missions (STMs) in over forty nations of the world, spanning three decades. These STMs have included multiple trips to North Africa (prior to 9/11 and once before the Arab Spring), numerous missions across the UK with different teams, three months in South-East Asia, numerous countries and cities across Europe, weeks of evangelism in Britain, six and a half months in Africa (along the East Coast), and three and a half months in Asia (including nearly two months in China). *Short-Term Missions, A Christian Guide to STMs* has been written from first-hand experience, as a participant, a host, and as a leader.

This book will aid you on your STM, whether you are an individual exploring the options (at home or abroad) or a church leader planning to take a group. You may have two weeks or a month free or be taking a gap year; you may be drawn towards a particular people group or country, or are just looking for the right mission organization to join. This book will assist you in areas of need: who to go with, how to finance it, what to pack, where to go, what to do, how to plan a STM, working with the locals, cultural and language issues etc. and will guide you through the STM process, before, during and when you return home, with firm foundations in the Word of God.

The book is largely written in a style that addresses the STM-er (a student or participant), but leaders and pastors can draw upon all the information shared, whilst specific leader issues are directly addressed. In some chapters, the author refers to 'we,' this is himself and any other members of the STM team whom he was travelling with or leading. Monies mentioned are in British pound sterling and American dollars at the exchange rate of £1 = $1.6 US dollars. (In 2017 due to BREXIT the exchange rate is £1 to $1.3).

The author would like to think that your STM would not be your last, but, by the grace of God, a stepping-stone as you listen to the call of God, be obedient to the Holy Spirit's promptings and follow in the Master's footsteps towards the fulfilment of the Great Commission, to the glory of God and exaltation of Jesus Christ.

Mathew Backholer
Co-founder of ByFaith Media

Chapter 1

Short-Term Missions and the Great Commission

Jesus said, "Go into all the world and preach the Gospel to every creature" (Mark 16:15).

Have you ever heard the following question or asked it yourself, "Why should I go on a short-term mission (STM)?" The simple answer is because Jesus told us to, "Go into all the world and preach the Good News to all nations" – this is the Great Commission and we can all participate if we go on a STM.

The Great Commission is not a request to be slotted into a busy schedule of our own life's pleasure and desires, but a command to be obeyed, and STMs help us work towards that aim. How will people hear the Good News if we do not go and tell them about it, showing them the love of Christ in action? If we do not go on a STM soon, when will we, if ever at all?

Why Go on a STM?

There are many reasons why people go on a STM and some are better than others. Let's take a look at them.

- The Call – to go.
- Concerned – for the lost.
- The Command – be obedient.
- Desire for the fulfilment of the Great Commission – "Go and make disciples of all nations..." (Matthew 28:19).
- Compassion – on those who have never heard.
- Compelled – 'Woe [intense mournfulness] is me if I do not preach the Gospel' (1 Corinthians 9:16).
- Escaping from problems or heartache at home.
- Gap year – often between college and university.
- To evangelise or civilise! Though the former is correct.
- Adventure – to see new places and time out from the routine.

STMs can be Life changing

STMs change not only the ones to whom they serve, but the person who goes. A mission trip is part of the college of life, it aids Christian discipleship, is educational and opens the world to others in far greater need than ourselves. It makes us think less of self and more of others, less of my problems and more on my blessings. It personally challenges us to pray for and to give more towards the

Great Commission at home and abroad and makes it personal, rather than distant. If you are overweight, you may also lose a few pounds or kilograms; so that cannot be bad! It has been good for me!

> A short-term mission trip not only assists and can change the lives of those whom you serve, but can be life changing for the those who went and served.

What you can Learn on your STM
- The generosity of those who have so little.
- About yourself, what is important and what is not, and what you can live without.
- About others, their needs, concerns, language, lifestyles and culture.
- Insights into your own culture and other cultures.
- Your strengths, weaknesses, character (the good, the neutral and the bad), and your giftings, talents and deficiencies.
- The importance of evangelism, world missions (at home and abroad) and the worldwide body of Christ.
- A greater love for Jesus, the importance of the Holy Spirit to empower and the Father heart of God.
- That "church" is done differently in other cultures with local expressions of worship and preaching.
- The importance to read and apply the truths of the Holy Bible. Memorisation of key Scriptures (especially evangelistic ones) are beneficial when sharing the Good News and will be recalled from your memory.
- The world is bigger than you thought and very diverse.
- Working together as a team and having individual responsibilities and duties.
- Your STM can be the start of God's bigger plan for your life – perhaps your future vocation, an adjustment of priorities, evaluation of finances, giftings and talents or taking your eyes off self and looking to the needs of others – the possibilities are endless.

> William Carey, missionary to India and the Father of Modern Missions said, "Few people know what may be done till they try and persevere in what they undertake."

The Great Commission
Jesus' parting Words to His disciples, before He ascended into heaven, revealed His most passionate desire to reach the lost – the

Great Commission – "Go therefore and make disciples of all nations..." (Matthew 28:19). This very important message which was entrusted to them was to be passed on from generation to generation (being practically outworked and fulfilled) because Jesus came to 'seek and to save' those who are lost (Luke 19:10), for 'there is no other name under heaven given among men by which we must be saved' (Acts 4:12).

God's love for mankind is immense and is revealed in John 3. 'For God so loved the world that He gave His only begotten Son, that whoever believes in Him should not perish but have everlasting life. For God did not send His Son into the world to condemn the world, but that the world through Him might be saved. He who believes in Him is not condemned, but he who does not believe is condemned already' (John 3:16-18). Jesus came to heal the broken-hearted, to bind up their wounds and to set the captives free, because the Spirit of the Lord was upon Him to preach the Good News to the poor (Luke 4:18-19) and we are called to follow in His footsteps.

Short-term missions are a great way to be part of the Great Commission. Those that go often use their holiday/vacation time, take a gap year or go outside of term time when schools, colleges and universities have finished for the term/semester.

The disciples were commissioned to preach and teach about the Kingdom of God; to proclaim the Good News of salvation, to make disciples, to cast out demons, to heal the sick and raise the dead (Matthew 28:18-20 and Mark 16:15-18) – all in the mighty name of Jesus Christ, the Son of God, the Saviour of the world. These commands of Jesus Christ, spoken nearly two thousand years ago are just as binding to us as to the early disciples. They are passed from one generation to the next until every tribe and tongue has heard the glad tidings – 'as a witness to all nations' and then, and only then, will Jesus come again (see Matthew 24:14, Revelation 5:9 and Revelation 7:9). However, Peter in relation to the Day of the Lord (the second coming of Jesus Christ), reiterated that we have our part to play – our responsibility and duty towards mankind. God is 'longsuffering towards us, not willing that any should perish but that all should come to repentance' and that we should be 'looking for and *hastening* the coming of the day of God' (2 Peter 3:9-12).

Jesus said, "All authority has been given to Me in heaven and on earth. Go therefore and make disciples of all the nations, baptising them in the name of the Father and of the Son and of the Holy Spirit, teaching them to observe all things that I have commanded you; and lo, I am with you always, even to the end of the age" (Matthew 28:18-20).

Mission Related Scriptures

- 'I have not hidden Your righteousness within my heart; I have declared Your faithfulness and Your salvation; I have not concealed Your loving kindness and Your truth from the great congregation' (Psalm 40:10).
- 'The dark places of the earth are full of the habitation of cruelty' (Psalm 74:20), this is why the Light of Christ must shine in the dark places!
- '...In that day there shall be a root of Jesse, who shall stand as a banner to the people; for the Gentiles shall seek Him...' (Isaiah 11:10).
- Thus says the Lord God, "When I say to the wicked, 'You shall surely die,' and you give him no warning, nor speak to warn the wicked from his wicked way, to save his life, that same wicked man shall die in his iniquity; but his blood I will require at your hand" (Ezekiel 3:18).
- The apostle Paul declared to the Ephesian elders that he 'kept back nothing that was helpful, but proclaimed it.' He was 'innocent of the blood of all men' because he did 'not shun to declare the whole counsel of God.' For three years he warned them night and day with tears (Acts 20:20-27, 31).
- Jesus said, "Go out into the highways and hedges [byways] and compel them to come in, that My house may be filled" (Luke 14:23).
- Jesus said, "...I chose you and appointed you that you should go forth and bear fruit and that your fruit should remain" (John 15:16).
- Jesus said, "...As the Father has sent Me, I also send you" (John 20:21).
- Jesus said, "...You shall be witnesses to Me in Jerusalem and in all Judea and Samaria and to the end of the earth" (Acts 1:8).

Contrasting Prophecies Paraphrased – Darkness and Light

- Magic spell and sorceries, astrologers and stargazers who make predictions every month, the fire will burn them up. They cannot save you and they cannot save themselves from the power of the flames! (Isaiah 47:12-15).
- How beautiful on the mountains are the feet of those who bring the good news, all the ends of the earth will see the salvation of God (Isaiah 52:7-10).

Chapter 2

To Go or not to Go on a STM

'The Lord gave the Word; great was the company of those who proclaimed it' (Psalm 68:11).

A large number of the characters of the Bible went on short-term missions (STMs), though, back then, it was known as a mission from God, a directive to go here, do that, or speak to such and such a person the Word of the Lord. Isaiah, Jeremiah, Ezekiel and Jonah are perhaps the best known within the Old Testament.

Within the New Testament, we have several more characters of which Jesus was the greatest. Jesus the Son of God was the greatest missionary who ever walked this earth, because He left His familiar surroundings of heaven and came to earth. He identified with the people He lived with and moved amongst. Jesus began His extensive ministry of training with twelve handpicked disciples. These core men were with Him from the beginning. When Jesus sent the twelve disciples out on their first STM He sent them in pairs, "He began to send them out two by two and gave them power over unclean spirits" (Mark 6:7). Jesus also sent the seventy out on a STM (Luke 10:1).

The reason people go on STMs is primarily to obey the command of Jesus, the Great Commission (Matthew 28:18-20 and Mark 16:15-18).[1] The question has been asked on many occasion, "Can anybody go on a STM trip?" Jesus said, "Go..." but people may have natural limitations or a disability that may make it very difficult in some places, whilst other people who are fully-abled may be a liability. Age, as well as existing health issues can be a factor in some places and these should be discussed with your doctor and any mission organization or church before you depart. Maturity in Christ (or lack of it) can also be a major consideration.

God can use anybody who is willing to go on a STM as it is not your ability, but your availability. There is an open call from God to all believers in Christ to be a part of His Great Commission and that includes giving *all* of yourself to God (Romans 12:1-2), so as to be able to respond to the call of God, "Who will go?" (Isaiah 6:8) or, "Who will stand in the gap?" in prayer (Ezekiel 22:30). The apostle Paul wrote: 'Woe is me if I do not preach the Gospel' (1 Corinthians 9:16). He intended to visit Asia Minor on a STM but had a vision, a calling to Macedonia, where he saw a man pleading, "Come and help us" (Acts 16:6-10) and so he went.

There are many reasons why some people think that they cannot go on a STM. For some it is: "I'm too young, I'm still at High School, I'm too poor, I'm not ordained, I have never preached or given my testimony, I have no qualifications or I'm useless."

Jeremiah was called by God as a young man and said, "Ah, Lord God! Behold I cannot speak, for I am a youth." But the Lord said, "Do not say, 'I am a youth,' for you shall go to all whom I send you...do not be afraid of their faces for I am with you..." (Jeremiah 1:6-7).

The apostle Paul wrote to Timothy: 'Let no one despise your youth, but be an example to the believers in word, in conduct, in love, in spirit, in faith, in purity' (1 Timothy 4:12).

Some of the twelve disciples were fishermen but they had no certificate from the Guild of Fishermen, whilst Peter and John were noted as 'uneducated and untrained,' yet those who heard them preach 'marvelled...[and] realised that they had been with Jesus' (Acts 4:13). The disciples had not been ordained by a denomination, but had been commissioned by Jesus to "Go" and they did, and saw great things for the glory of God.

It is important that none of us look down upon ourselves (or on others) and you should not let anyone look down upon you because of your age or gender. If you have a testimony (Jesus has saved me), a call and a willing heart to go on STM then you are qualified.

George Verwer, founder of Operation Mobilisation said, "The devil would love to convince you that all this mission stuff isn't for you. The devil is a liar and you know it!"

Family Ties and Responsibilities

There are those with a family to look after and you cannot just run off and leave your spouse, the children, or ageing parents (if you are their carer) to go on a STM. If you are married, is your spouse in full support? If you have children what will happen to their schooling if they come with you, or if they stay home with one parent? What about pre-existing health issues? A person may have a work commitment which delays their departure. If you are at High School or College etc. don't go when you should be in class. Wait for term/recess time, often during summer vacation.

If you are in debt and struggle to pay off your loans and credit cards then your financial obligations will hinder you going on a STM; especially if you have missed mortgage or rent payments. The Bible tells us that we are to 'owe no one anything, except to love one another' (Romans 13:8). You are duty bound to pay off your debts as agreed in stages (often monthly repayments), as defaulting on your agreement is not the best way forward. Creditors will come down hard on any default and this could land you in trouble.

If you are taking a year out and have a student loan then the repayment issues will vary because you have zero income. If you have made bad financial choices in the past, is it right to get people to part with their money (individuals or your church) for you to go on a STM (see Luke 16:10 and Luke 19:11-27). We must all take responsibility for our actions.[2] Do you need to sell your sports car to part-finance your STM, because other models are cheaper: to insure, to purchase, maintain, with greater fuel/gas economy.

It is also advisable not to finance your STM on borrowed money because you'll have to pay it back with interest! Where God guides, He provides, as God pays His own invoices.

'As the eyes of servants look to the hand of their masters, as the eyes of a maid to the hand of her mistress, so our eyes look to the Lord our God...' (Psalm 123:2).

Health Issues and Disability

Do you or any members of your team have any pre-existing health issues? Leaders beware! The medicine may not be available where you are going on your STM and the nearest hospital may be days away. Before you depart on your STM, stock up on your prescription medicines and keep them in their original packaging. For some medicines you may want a letter from your doctor, because at customs you may be perceived as a travelling pharmacist!

A disability may not eliminate those who desire to go on a STM, but certain locations may not be appropriate. Some mission organizations or agencies may not be able to give the assistance they need or feel unable to accept their application.

Whatever your circumstances, everyone can still pray for world missions, others are able to go on a STM and others will be able to give financial support (Matthew 9:35-38). For some, their obstacles in preventing them from participating on a STM may dissolve over time as God moves in mysterious ways. With God, nothing is impossible. Do not squeeze God into your plans, fit into His!

'Now in the church that was at Antioch there were certain prophets and teachers.... As they ministered to the Lord and fasted, the Holy Spirit said, "Now separate to Me Barnabas and Saul for the work which I have called them"' (Acts 13:1-2).

Chapter 3

Good Stewardship

Jesus said, "My food is to do the will of Him who sent Me, and to finish His work. ...Look at the fields, for they are already white unto harvest. And he who reaps receives wages and gathers fruit for eternal life, so that he who reaps may rejoice together.... 'One sows another reaps' " (John 4:34-37).

A minority of Christians claim that short-term missions (STMs) are a waste of finances. There are many and varied reasons why some hold to this point of view, but can we quantify a price for a soul? 'For the redemption of their souls is costly...' (Psalm 49:8a). We should be wise and good stewards of our resources, and if we are *only* focussing on development aid then it is understandable why the argument, "waste of finances" is heard from some quarters.

Some would say that money spent on STMs takes essential resources away from traditional mission organizations or diverts funds away from a missionary who was sent out by their local church. This is often not true as new money is *released* and not diverted from other causes. In reality, new funds are *created* to finance those who go on a STM which otherwise would have been spent on other things: a car, a holiday/vacation, new TV or mobile/cell phone, and without the STM, would never have filtered into the mission field. Research reveals that those who have gone on STMs are more likely to pray more and to give more towards world missions than those who have never gone, so STMs increases the level of financial giving!

The exception may be if the church finances the STM in its entirety, which personally, I think is unwise. If it costs the STM-er nothing, he or she will generally give less of themselves than if it came out of their own wallet or purse, and not appreciate the hard toil in obtaining those funds. There is always a danger that those with an adventurous spirit and those who wish to take a two-week break or a gap year, will always jump at the chance of a STM when the financial responsibility is not upon them.

Nobody bats an eyelid when a family from the church flies off to another continent on a two-week holiday/vacation – in fact it is deemed quite normal. The holiday of mum (mom), dad and two children over six years of age would have cost a minimum of £3,000 ($4,800), but could be considerably higher. So is it reasonable to say STMs are a waste of finances, whereas they are of Kingdom value and a holiday/vacation is not necessarily so? Rest and relaxation is good to recharge our physical batteries, but there is overindulgence and some people insist on two holidays a year.

There are some who say that the finances used for a STM could be better stewarded to produce a greater harvest in other areas. That may be so, but have the proponents of this belief and their church used that same amount of money and produced a harvest or is it just an untested theory? How many souls were saved within their church building last year and are still true to the faith now? How much did the evangelistic campaign cost (how many months of preparation were involved) and what fruit was born – if any?

A STM is not about statistics, but it is a life changing experience and an investment into the Kingdom of God. STMs can lead to long-term fruit in the person who has gone – praying for missions, financially supporting and mission mobilizing (encouraging others and raising awareness).

Some full-time missionaries say that a team of STM-ers can cause problems and I don't deny that, but even the Scriptures declare, 'Where no oxen are, the trough is clean, but much increase comes by the strength of an ox' (Proverbs 14:4), and who is to say that these same missionaries have not caused problems? We all make mistakes; it's part of life and let us learn from them!

STM teams reveal the principle of synergism, where the combined power of two increases, as opposed to an individual going it alone on the same objective, because 'two are better than one, because they have a good reward for their labour.' 'And a threefold cord is not quickly broken' (Ecclesiastes 4:9, 12).

> Someone once said, "No one ever said that short-term missions are the way to evangelise the world, but they are a good way to get started!"

Age of Globalisation

We live in an age of globalisation, whereas in previous centuries; missionaries had to stay in one place for several years to learn the language, to build a home, to till the land and to interact with the people who were as alien to the missionaries, as they were to the locals. In the twenty-first century you can go to most countries and find English speaking people. At least half the world have access to a mail box or the internet and how many people use a smartphone to communicate? Training materials, tracts, Bibles and portions of Gospels are available in more than two thousand languages of the world and so the time needed in one place is very different for a STM-er as opposed to one who had been called to give their entire life to a particular field of service. Both long-term and short-term workers are valuable to the Kingdom of God and its advancement. STMs in no way replaces the traditional missionary but are often there to assist them in their ministry for a shorter period and to open to the STM-er the world of missions and sometimes, God's will for their lives. For many full-time missionaries their job function is to establish or plant a local church (translate the Bible etc.), whereas STMs are designed to support local churches and to work in partnership with them.

The Bible speaks of sowers, reapers and builders, and in the Kingdom of God we all have our part to play (see Matthew 13:3-9, John 4:37-38 and 1 Corinthians 3:3-17). The apostle Paul wrote: 'I planted, Apollos watered, but God gave the increase. So neither he who plants is anything, nor he who waters, but God who gives the increase. Now he who plants and he who waters are one, and each one will receive his own reward according to his own labour' (1 Corinthians 3:6-8).

'...The king's business required haste' (1 Samuel 21:8b).

Without Excuse

The Bible explains to us that creation is a witness for the existence of God (Romans 2:20-21), but non-Christians (the unsaved) also need a living witness to Jesus Christ, someone to tell them the Good News. '...How shall they hear without a preacher? And how shall they preach unless they are sent?' (Romans 10:14-15). Will you support STMs (by your money, prayers and your self) as an investment into the Kingdom of God?

Evan Roberts of the Welsh Revival (1904-1905) said, "How shall the heathen [unevangelised] warm himself by the eternal fires of God's love, if we not give the money for the fuel?"[1]

'For the message of the cross is foolishness to those who are perishing, but to us who are being saved it is the power of God' (1 Corinthians 1:18).

Chapter 4

Short-Term Mission Motives

'Every way of a man is right in his own eyes, but the Lord weighs the hearts' (Proverbs 21:2).

Many people go on a short-term mission (STM) because they have received a direct Word from the Lord – they are called of God. God may not grab your attention like Moses at the burning bush (Exodus 3:1-4) or Elijah at the mountain of God where an earthquake and then a fire got his attention (1 Kings 19:11-12), but God spoke through a still small voice. During your quiet time (prayer and Bible reading), God may have spoken to you about the needs of a certain people group or country, or you feel burdened or concerned about those who have never heard the Good News. Others have been reading a Christian book or magazine, watching a documentary on television or online and they just 'know' that God is leading them towards a certain place (country or people) as something just 'jumps out' and grabs their attention. Your church may be organising a STM and you feel that God is prompting you to sign up, or a visiting preacher or missionary has highlighted the needs of a certain area or people and it speaks deeply to your heart. If you are leading a STM, then you are also seeking God for His will and reading this for advice.

People can be fickle, the heart is deceptive and there are many reasons why people want to go on a STM, some are honourable and some are not honourable. For some it is: To make them feel good, frustrations at home/college or work, for adventure (itchy feet), to look good, to delay their further education, to put off the inevitable of getting a job, the advice of their pastor or youth leader, to help others, to win the lost, to serve, to obey the command of Jesus Christ, "Go...", or the call of God etc.

> 'All a man's ways seem innocent to him, but motives are weighed by the Lord' (Proverbs 16:2), NIV.

It is important that each individual should know why they are going on a STM. If you know why you are going and what you will be doing, then your mind will be made up to see the mission through to the end (regardless of the ups and downs or any bumps that you may encounter along the way), then your expectations and realisations should be closely matched. Fear is a normal part of life, however some fear is rational and some is irrational. In regards to STMs, worst than fear of the unknown, is the fear of being paralyzed into doing nothing and then spending the rest of your life with, "What if?" being run through your mind from one week to the next on a perpetual loop. If you do not go, you will never know, but you will always regret the fact that you allowed the opportunity to pass you by, and the opportunity of a lifetime must be seized during the lifetime of the opportunity. If you don't go – you'll never know!

J. Hudson Taylor, after he founded the China Inland Mission was giving advice to a group of pioneers who were under his leadership. He reminded the group that there are several different ways of working for God. He said, "One is to make the best plans we can and carry them out to the best of our ability. This may be better than working without a plan, but it is by no means the best way of serving our Master. Or, having carefully laid our plans and determined to carry them through, we may ask God to help us and to prosper us in connection with them. Yet another way of working is to begin with God; to ask His plans and to offer ourselves to carry out His purposes."[1]

As a missionary in China, J. Hudson Taylor, wrote to a friend who needed guidance: 'Light will no doubt be given you. Do not forget, however, in seeking more, the importance of walking according to the light you have. If you feel called to the work, do not be anxious about the time and way. He will make it plain...I desire increasingly to leave all my affairs in the hands of God, who alone can and who assuredly will, lead us aright if humbly and in faith we seek His aid.

'...I urge on you...the importance of seeking guidance from God for yourself personally apart from the movements of others. ...But let us seek to see our own way clearly in the light of His will and then in trial and perplexity we shall be 'steadfast, unmoveable,' not having trusted to an arm of flesh. The Lord guide and bless you and give you ever to lean unshaken on His faithfulness.'[2]

Godly Counsel

Godly sound biblical advice alongside wise counsel can be sought from a mature Christian, such as your pastor or youth leader etc. for your STM. Pray for wisdom and for God's will.

- 'Where there is no counsel, the people fall, but in the multitude of counsellors there is safety' (Proverbs 11:14).
- 'The first one to plead his cause seems right until his neighbour comes and examines him' (Proverbs 18:17).
- 'Every purpose is established by counsel...' (Proverbs 20:18).
- "...Ask in prayer, believing, you will receive" (Matthew 21:22).

- 'If any of you lacks wisdom, let him ask of God, who gives to all liberally and without reproach, and it will be given to him' (James 1:5).

Steps of Obedience for God's will to be Revealed
- Move in step with God, not too quick or too slow (Psalm 32:9 and Galatians 5:25).
- Fear God and He will teach you the way to go (Psalm 25:12). C.f. Proverbs 1:7a, Proverbs 8:13a and Proverbs 9:10.
- God's timing is always critical and essential for any work (Acts 16:5-10 and Acts 19:8-10). C.f. Acts 13:1-5.
- Trust God entirely (Psalm 37:4-7, Psalm 37:22, Proverbs 3:5-7 and Matthew 6:25-34).
- Yield yourself fully to God that you will know His will (Romans 12:1-2 and 2 Corinthians 5:15). C.f. John 4:34.
- And remember to obey God completely when He makes His will known to you (Acts 16:10).

Multitudes of people have never heard the Good News, yet the command to preach the Gospel to every creature has never been cancelled. The question is: "What am I doing about it?" Are we constrained by the love of Christ and the hope of His coming to obey His last command?

The Bottom Line
STMs help build character and are life-changing experiences because not only the hearer or receiver is blessed, but the giver as well. A STM can broaden one's horizons, it can open our eyes to see how the other half live and how well-off we really are. A STM can be an adventure or time out between studies (or a job) and hopefully those that go, will go with the right motives and the right heart.

The person concerned, may only ever go on one STM, but they will never forget the experience. Who is to say that they will not be more active in home evangelism, raising mission support for those on the field (both financially and in prayer), encouraging other members of their church to 'go' and become intercessors for the nations?

A prayer of King Asa, "...O Lord our God, for *we rest on You*, and *in Your name we go* against this multitude. O Lord, You are our God; do not let man prevail against You!" (2 Chronicles 14:11).

'Let us hear the conclusion of the matter: Fear God and keep His commandments, for this is the whole duty of man' (Ecclesiastes 12:13). Jesus said, "Go into all the world and preach the Gospel to every creature" (Mark 16:15).

Chapter 5

The Good News or Good Works

Jesus said, "Go into all the world and preach the Gospel to every creature..." (Mark 16:15), "That repentance and remission of sins should be preached in His name to all nations..." (Luke 24:47).

The world of short-term missions (STMs) is as long as it is wide and deep, with hundreds of organizations offering thousands of opportunities in a multitude of destinations in a large variety of capacities from sharing the Good News to doing good deeds; evangelising, preaching, praying or helping others. The major types of humanitarian and development aid are: Education, working with children, building or feeding programmes, hydration (boreholes and making water wells), medical work, agricultural, mechanical maintenance, sport programmes and prison ministry. You may be looking for an organization or planning a STM. The following is what you can do on your STM.
- Preach the Gospel – sharing the Good News about Jesus Christ.
- Humanitarian Aid – helping people with their immediate needs.
- Development Aid – assisting humankind in areas of development.
- Prayer Team – praying around locations and districts.
- Any combination of the above, however aid work is not necessarily Christian work, but can be a deviation from what you should be doing.

Preach the Gospel
The primary concern of the Great Commission is to proclaim the Good News, which can split into many directions as part of evangelism, church planting and building up the body of Christ (teaching) etc. It is based on the commands of Jesus Christ:
- "Go therefore and make disciples of all nations...teaching them to observe all things I have commanded you..." (Matthew 28:18-20).
- "Go into all the world and preach the Gospel to every creature..." (Mark 16:15).
- "As the Father has sent Me, I also send you..." (John 20:21).

- "That repentance and remission of sins should be preached in His name to all nations..." (Luke 24:47).
- "You shall receive power when the Holy Spirit has come upon you and you shall be witnesses to Me in Jerusalem and in all Judea and Samaria and to the end of the earth" (Acts 1:8).

> Go not to those who need you, but to those who need you the most – John Wesley, founder of Methodism.

Humanitarian Aid

Humanitarian aid is concerned with the interests and welfare of humans – helping those who are in immediate need. To save lives, alleviate suffering and maintain human dignity. Christians should support Christian humanitarian organizations that honour the Lord Jesus Christ; not secular organizations that reject His Word and His complete healing of mind, soul and body. Development aid should involve giving someone a hand-up, rather than just a hand-out though in times of famine and war, a hand-out is often the only way.

- Feeding the poor, giving water to those that thirst, clothing the naked and visiting those in prison, "In as much as you did it to one of the least of these My brethren you did it to Me" (Matthew 25:35-46).
- Medical missions can be the only way into sensitive countries or into closed hearts. It is based on, "They will lay hands on the sick and they will recover" (Mark 16:18). This Scripture is based on Divine healing, which can go hand-in-hand.
- Education and feeding programmes. Jesus taught the people and fed the five and four thousand. In the case of the five thousand, Jesus, upon being told by His disciples to send the people away (to get lodgings and provisions) said, "You give them something to eat" (Luke 9:12-17).
- Visiting and assisting others. 'Pure and undefiled religion before God and the Father is this: to visit orphans and widows in their trouble, and to keep oneself unspotted from the world' (James 1:27).
- Love in action. 'But whoever has this world's goods and sees his brother in need, and shuts up his heart from him; how does the love of God abide in him? ...Let us not love in word or in tongue, but in deed and in truth' (1 John 3:17-18). This last verse is directed towards the family of God, assisting the brethren in their time of need, but still reiterates the biblical principle of love in action, which is universal to anyone. 'If your enemy is hungry, give him bread to eat and

if he is thirsty, give him water to drink' (Proverbs 25:21). See also Matthew 5:44 and Matthew 19:19.

> The apostle Paul wrote to the Church at Corinth: 'Awake to righteousness, and do not sin; *for some do not have the knowledge of God*. I speak this to your shame' (1 Corinthians 15:34). And '...Woe is me if I do not preach the gospel!' (1 Corinthians 9:16b).

Widows and Orphans

Christian aid and love for mankind also incorporates God's love and concern for widows and orphans (see Exodus 22:22, and Psalm 68:5). In some cultures, it is the man's responsibility (or the only person who is permitted) to provide for his household and when he is absent, economic problems and hardships can exist for the remainder of the family. See also Psalm 83:3-4, James 1:27 and 1 Timothy 5:3-16).

Prayer Team

A prayer team or an intercessory prayer team is a group of Christians, often from the same church, who go to specific places to pray and intercede. Sometimes they work alongside missionaries whilst at other times, they go and 'spy-out the land' praying on stony and hard soil to try and soften the ground before a STM team arrives. This ministry of prayer and intercession can either be an underrated or an overrated ministry with some team members knowing what they are doing, whilst others have not got a clue, yet think they do! Biblical characters such as Abraham, Moses, Jeremiah, Isaiah, Ezekiel, Daniel, Hosea, Jesus and the apostle Paul were all intercessors alongside many others. See Isaiah 62:6-7, Ezekiel 3:17-19, Romans 8:26-27, Ephesians 3:10, Ephesians 6:12-17 and 1 Timothy 2:1-4.

Key Scriptural Principles for Answered Prayer
- Confess all known sin (Psalm 66:18 and Proverbs 28:13).
- What is your motive in praying for —? (James 4:3).
- Is God glorified through your prayers? (John 16:23).
- Is it a need or a want? (Matthew 6:9-13).
- Is it God's will? (Matthew 6:10 and 1 John 5:14).
- Ask in Jesus' name (John 16:23).
- Believe and have faith (Mark 11:24 and Luke 11:9).
- Corporate prayer (Matthew 18:19), and in unity with others (Psalm 133 and Ephesians 4:3).
- Be persistent in your prayers (Luke 18:1).

Chapter 6

Mission Considerations

Jesus said, "You shall receive power when the Holy Spirit has come upon you; and you shall be witnesses to Me in Jerusalem, and in all Judea and Samaria, and to the end of the earth" (Acts 1:8).

You may have heard the call to go on your short-term mission (STM), but you also need to be in the right place at the right time. Like Isaiah, you may be able to say, "Here I am! Send me" (Isaiah 6:8) – but may not have the faintest where to go, with whom, or know the duration of the STM. However, with some basic research and waiting upon God in prayer, the will of the Lord will be revealed and He can give you perfect peace about the entire situation. Some factors to consider are:

Go with Whom?
- Mission Organization – a specialist in STMs.
- Part of a church mission – youth group or a team of varied ages. You may be the leader who is planning the STM.
- Independent STM – with friend(s) or church associate(s).

Work in Association and have Objectives
With all of the above options, you may work in association with a local church or ministry, orphanage, school, building programme or a missionary. If you are a leader then your team can either go on a STM with some defined objectives of: preaching the Good News, distribution of Christian literature, some form of humanitarian or development aid or any combination. You may work with a host church or missionary from within the country you are going to.

Leaders must also remember that the missionary you may be working alongside (with your STM team) has their own duties to fulfill and so may not be able to supervise or be present at every meeting. The missionary may have permitted your team to stay at his or her home or have arranged meetings for you out of courtesy or under obligation to his or her denomination or superior. This does not make the missionary, your maid, cook, driver or personal assistant. Whilst they are probably delighted with your presence and will assist you as much as they can, respect their home, mission compound and/or headquarters, as well as their responsibilities, time and duties. Don't be a burden, but a blessing! Be a servant to them and not a guest. Be so helpful and good that once you have gone home, they look forward to the next STM team's arrival.

If there is just two or more of you on your STM (who are not part of a mission organization) then you may have no fixed-in-concrete plans and be entirely led of the Holy Spirit as an independent STM team. As you travel, you pray for Divine appointments and see what happens as you move from one place to the next, moving across a district, country (like Jesus and His disciples) or countries. However, you may also team up with a host church or organization in another country and work alongside or assist or support them with your labour and giftings. In relation to this book, much of what has been written in relation to independent STM teams also relates to church leaders planning to take a team. The only difference is one is sanctioned/commissioned by the local church or denomination and the other may not be.

In sensitive countries where evangelising is illegal (or to change one's faith), it is unwise to associate with a "missionary" as you may blow their cover. They may want no contact with independent STM-ers or STM teams. Some teams take in Christian literature and discreetly distribute them or act as an unofficial postal service!

Style of Your Mission
- One fixed location. This is a good way to have a firm foundation in a single area. You can build friendships with the local pastor, missionary, congregation and locals.
- Several locations within one country. This works well when in sensitive areas and you are distributing Christian materials, booklets, gospels, Bibles etc. Sometimes you need to be in and out of a town within days. If a member of the team gets caught by the authorities (often they are just told off and material is confiscated) then it is wise to move to another place, without telling local people where you are going. Different locations within the same country can also broaden one's horizons whilst the area and culture can be very different.
- Multiple towns across one country. You have to go from A to E (perhaps you fly in and out from different locations) and therefore can spend time in B, C and D.
- From country to country. Travelling from one country to another can be like going from one State to another. You may be working with the same denomination doing similar forms of mission work or have existing friends in Christian ministry whom you wish to learn from, to serve and to work alongside.

- Multiple countries – even across a continent. This is very uncommon, but similar to above. You may have other Christian objectives or wish to visit sites of historical Christian interest.

Be aware that a STM must have Christian objectives. To wander about aimlessly within a country (or countries), seeing all the sights and just soaking up the atmosphere sounds more like a travel adventure, rather than Christian focussed ministry. One man wanted to go on holiday and convinced himself that if he took a few tracts along, he could call it a STM!

Duration of Your Mission and the Timing
- Weeks, months or a year or more.
- The time of year to go, there is big difference between summer and winter and the dry and rainy seasons. These factors are irrelevant if you are spending a year in one place, but if it is from weeks to just a few months, then it can be a contributing factor to help hone the decision and to eliminate certain places or times of the year.
- If you are going to a sensitive area, (especially for independent STM-ers) be aware that different religions celebrate their own festivals and holidays/vacations with their various rituals, which can heighten their emotional excitement and possibly be a threat to you. Westerners are a target in certain areas of the world. Stay clear of mosques after Friday prayers.

The Time of Your Mission
If you are joining a mission organization for your STM then all the above factors will have already been considered, noted and worked into their programme. Two to three weeks is a good slot for many Christians considering a STM because of their vacation time. If you are a student, in between college or university then this period is extended and for some, can be a gap year. With many mission organizations the length of their missions vary, but one, three or six months is quite standard, as is the longer STM of one or two years, though many organization have STMs of just two to three weeks. Whilst your local church, or you and your friends can tailor-make a mission, sometimes, the cost of plane tickets can be a deciding factor as it is often cheaper to fly mid-week, rather than at the weekend.

Staying in one fixed location for a fixed period is easier than moving from place to place during the same amount of time.

The duration and time of your mission can be determined by many factors:

- Holiday/vacation – how long is my time off from work etc.?
- Term-time – school, college or university; when are they closed and for how long?
- National holidays/vacations – the locals go away, shops shut. For some locals it is family time and not a time for strangers, or a time for attending meetings or discussing spiritual matters which are unrelated to their own beliefs.
- High or low season – costs increase in the high season (at peak demand) and accommodation costs varies with supply and demand.
- Weather and climate – (summer, winter, dry or wet season?). Problems arise when the ministry is outside or during the agricultural seasons in rural areas when people work from dawn to dusk and beyond! Poor or hard weather will keep people off the streets (or public places) and away from special Christian meetings.
- The invitation – when (or if) you are invited to work with the local host church, mission or missionary.
- Family considerations – will you, your parents, spouse or child need certain medical help at designated times of the year? Is it available or too expensive? The quality, training, hygiene and equipment can vary.
- Special seasons – Christmas, Thanksgiving, Easter, Ramadan, Yom Kippur (though only one day), other religious festivals, special anniversary dates and national holidays (e.g. Chinese New Year) – from your own country or to where you are going, can hinder, disrupt, or enhance your mission plans. Flights are booked well in advance.

The World's Calendars and Time and Day

The world does not have a unified calendar which means that the calendar date, the time of day and year can all be measured differently depending on the country you are in. Crossing from one country to the next (or between States or districts) can change time zones. In some countries, the day begins at sunrise and not at one second past midnight as in the West. Do not book accommodation etc. by using only numerals, e.g. 7/09/17 can mean the seventh of September 2017 or the ninth of July 2017!

'The fruit of the righteous is a tree of life and he who wins souls is wise' (Proverbs 11:30).

Questions to Ask Yourself

To aid discernment, in prayerfully choosing where to go, whilst narrowing down the options ask yourself the following questions:

- What languages can I speak? Do I need to speak a certain language if I am to go to —? It is not always necessary (though very helpful) to know the language.
- What can I do and what specific skills do I have?
- What is the neediest place? The world is needy, but where would I best be suited?
- Where can I go and be effective – where is the harvest? Jesus said we should pray for more labourers to be sent out into the harvest and that the fields are white unto harvest (Matthew 9:37-38 and John 4:35-38).
- What time commitment am I able to give for my mission? Two weeks, two months, a year etc.?
- Can I cope with the climate? Most countries are seasonal. What about altitude or if I am based near volcanic ash – asthmatics beware!
- Do I have poor health? It can be dangerous to go to some countries where medical aid is much to be desired and the hospital could be several days drive away.
- Finances – how much savings do I have – can I use them? Or can I get enough money for the STM?

'My God shall supply all your need according to His riches in glory by Christ Jesus' (Philippians 4:19).

The Cost

It is not fair to consider a STM for a year if you expect your small church to finance you (when not even the pastor gets a wage) and especially if you have no savings of your own. However, faith should determine your venture and not your finances as God does not discriminate, He pays His own bills and where He guides He does provide!

If every individual who wants to go on a STM is able to come up with some of the money, then it helps them to get a sense of the cost and value of the STM. To earn and save money can be hard work, but it gives a sense of achievement and fulfilment. When the local church is also able to part-finance an individual (or part of the church's STM team), then this gives the congregation a sense of being a part of the team and belonging to a greater cause than just the local church. The church is investing into the Kingdom of God and is seeing the bigger picture of Christianity.

Chapter 7

Who To Go With

'I planted, Apollos watered, but God gave the increase. So neither he who plants is anything, nor he who waters, but God who gives the increase. Now he who plants and he who waters are one, and each one will receive his own reward according to his own labour' (1 Corinthians 3:6-8).

If you are going on a short-term mission (STM), you are going as a helper to serve others. Regardless of whom you go with (a mission organization, your church, or an independent STM – with two or more of you), the mission must not be confused with an all-inclusive holiday/vacation – or a holiday full stop, because you are going to work for the Lord.

Most STM organizations, where each mission exceeds several months will have an orientation programme, a week or two of training (or even longer) where you can meet other members of your team and receive some basic training before you depart. The more you learn before you depart, the easier it will be when you arrive. For other organizations, there may be a brief programme on your arrival, perhaps just a few hours.

Mission organizations serve in different countries and each has its weak and strong points. Some are more experienced than others and the costs vary considerably; as do their duration and locations. All of these factors need to be taken into consideration. MissionsNow.co.uk under its 'Mission Links' page has numerous mission organizations and their opportunities and lists agencies which fit people of varying ages and giftings, talents and skills, with various organizations working across the world, with STMs ranging from two weeks to two years.

Will the mission organization look after you – what is their code of practice or conduct? Any company or organization with a product will not downplay what is on offer, but mission agencies should show integrity in how they publish their opportunities and in what they offer. Inevitably, any organization will make mistakes, but ideally, they will learn from it, improve or correct certain features for future STM-ers, otherwise the organization will get a bad name and it will not survive. At other times, there are circumstances beyond their control, which affect STMs such as natural disasters, wars and terrorist attacks, which can cause delays, close roads or airports.

There is also equipment failure (breakdown of vehicles or the boiler) and all these events, alter the best of plans, which may delay departure from one place to another, close a door to certain areas of a country, or keep you from having a hot shower!

'...So it was that for a whole year they assembled with the church and taught a great many people. And the disciples were first called Christians at Antioch' (Acts 11:26).

A Common Vision and Beliefs
It is important that you share the same vision as the organization that you intend to work with – what is their mission statement? You (or they) may hold a particular theological bias which will cause contentions and some things which you believe in (and may have experienced, e.g. Christian healing) they may deny or disown. They may not permit a woman to preach and you want to, though in some cultures, it is not permissible for a woman to preach to a mixed congregation. On the other hand, you may not want to preach (or share your testimony) and it may be required!

If you have an evangelistic gift and frown on the social gospel (where only good deeds are performed without sharing the Good News), then some organizations are not for you. On the other hand, most organizations will not be holding evangelistic meetings night after night to thousands or even hundreds of people, be realistic in your expectations of your mission. Some organizations or churches may expect everyone, on at least one occasion to share their testimony at a church or other meeting and this is nothing to be afraid of. Other issues may evolve around:

- What you can or cannot wear: revealing clothing or no trousers (pants) for women.
- The time you begin in the morning or the time you have to be in bed or lights out.
- Relationships with the opposite sex.
- Your general appearance: style of clothing (e.g. not extreme), hair length, piercings, fleshies or tattoos etc.
- Headscarves for women: often in Islamic countries.
- Things you need to bring or are not permitted to.
- No mixed swimming and/or modest bathing costumes for men and women.
- Being accountable to the leadership team.
- There may be other rules that could apply to the mission organization or agency you are considering. Ask them.

Do thorough research before you decide to join any mission organization on a STM and pray for wisdom, discernment and guidance: that God will show you where He wants you in whatever country or district, with what organization and when. Look at their website and social media and read all their content if you are serious about joining a STM organization; especially the frequently asked questions (FAQ) page. Do you need to ask them to send you some literature? Do they have an open day near you? Ask questions via email, social media or phone (have your questions written down). Do you know of anyone else who has been with them – what was their experience like? What age range do they cater for? Do they have lower or upper age limits? Do they need any specialist skills or language requirements?

Most organized mission agencies and ministries will generally stay in a single location. Some will move to a different area just once or twice within the year. The latter approach will broaden the STM-er's horizon, bring added experience and will reveal the different needs amongst those to whom they are serving. The former helps people to concentrate all their efforts in one place, making it easier to see the 'fruit' of one's labour. In the free enrolment in the college of life, we should all be students, ready and eager to learn from others.

If you are going with a mission organization or church, then they will tell you the exact price of the mission and what it covers and just as importantly, what it does not cover. Often excursions for days off are optional and some organizations do allow their "workers" weekends off in which they may not be permitted to leave the area. As with all things, it is always better to find out what is expected and what is not permitted before you sign on the dotted line and pay your deposit. Read the small print!

If your church is making a sizable contribution towards your STM, is the pastor, head of missions or the mission board in agreement that this particular mission organization is for you? Crossing a denominational line is a step too far for some churches.

You must have a high level of confidence in the mission organization that you are going to join for your STM. Pray for God's guidance and perfect will for your STM.

Going with your Church

Many larger churches have regular STMs to various parts of the world, where they link up with local churches or organizations and annually or biannually renew friendships and minister within another country, State or county. There are many advantages of going on a STM with your church; you know the people you are travelling with, you hold common beliefs and you trust the ones you are going with. On the other hand, it might be your church's first STM, so expect the unexpected and your leader may be inexperienced, but life is a learning curve and we can learn from our mistakes and those of others. Sometimes the pastor or youth leader will join the STM team but another person is the designated leader, simply because he or she has the experience in this area. Always show the greatest of respect to leaders.

Maybe you are considering taking a team on a STM from your church and have never been yourself. If so, start small and embrace the opportunity to help enrich the lives of others – those whom you will serve, and for every member of the team (including yourself) as you learn in the college of life. Go to a 'safe' country or to another State/county.

Jesus said, "Do not worry, saying, 'What shall we eat?' or 'What shall we drink?' or... 'What shall we wear?'... But seek first the Kingdom of God and His righteousness, and all these things shall be added unto you" (Matthew 6:31, 33).

Independent STMs

In the Old Testament, prophets went from place to place declaring the Word of the Lord. Jonah reluctantly went on a cross-cultural mission to Nineveh, to a people group from another nation. Jesus and His disciples travelled from one town to the next proclaiming the Kingdom of God, calling people to repent, healing people of physical and spiritual infirmities and teaching them about the things of God. The apostle Paul (also known as Saul) was another great example of an independent STM-er who travelled to multiple destinations on his mission trips, with different helpers, staying varying lengths of time in one place to the next.

The independent STM-er will encounter more incidences that are varied and perhaps more problems than one who joins an organization. The Christian centre, mission compound or the local hotel may be great; but the monotony of an isolated location can also bring about its own problems, especially when team members have fallen out or if there is no place for privacy.

As noted earlier, within this book, what applies to an independent STM team also relates to a leader planning to take a team.

Charles Caleb Colton (1780–1832) wrote: 'Those who visit foreign nations, but associate only with their own country-men, change their climate, but not their customs. They see new meridians, but the same men; and with heads as empty as their pockets, return home with travelled bodies, but untravelled minds.'

Chapter 8

Guidance from Heaven

'Trust in the Lord with all your heart and lean not on your own understanding; in all your ways acknowledge Him and He will direct your paths' (Proverbs 3:5-6).

From a human perspective, we have looked at various things to consider in the previous chapters and whilst we can whittle out certain destinations or times of the year, eliminate some mission organizations or agencies and weigh certain factors into the equation, we have to be in the will of the Lord. If we go outside of the will of the Lord then we will not be able to get the maximum benefit for our limited time on our short-term mission (STM).

The world is a needy place and the fields are white unto harvest, but most people can only work in one field (Matthew 9:38 and John 4:35). The question is: "What is the field of labour for my STM?" The need of an area does not necessarily constitute a call for you to go there and minister, though it may be a deciding factor.

A choice between right or wrong is often not difficult for a disciple to make, but when the choice is between two right things then we may need some extra help, seek godly counsel and pray. The timing of a STM is as important as all the other factors. You could join the right mission organization for your STM, to go to the correct country or area, but the timing also has to be perfect. Don't run ahead of God or lag behind in His call for your participation on your STM.

We can do many things for God without Him, and He may even bless it, but when we do what He says, then He will anoint us for the task to bear fruit for His glory (John 15:7-8). There is a big difference between God blessing a work and God anointing it, compare Acts 16:6-10 with Acts 19:10.

God can speak to you in many ways: He may directly say, "Go to ——," or "Join with —— mission organization." God may burden your heart, or open your eyes to the needs of a certain people group or ministry job. He may impress upon you a certain STM organization or your church may invite you to join the team (they may ask you to lead it) and you have the peace of God that it is His will. You may have the skills that fill a gap in a team or a natural disaster occurs and you want to go and assist in immediate humanitarian or development aid.

Guidance from God

God has promised to guide the believer, but there are conditions that need to be met, but they always revolve around obedience to God! See Psalm 25:9, Psalm 32:8-9, Proverbs 28:9, Isaiah 42:6 and John 16:13. If you are already in employment or studies, do not hand in your notice unless you know it to be the will of God. Immediately quitting is probably not from God. Take godly advice from your pastor, youth leader or a mature Christian friend (someone who walks close with God). Sometimes a desire can be wishful thinking, or the devil trying to confuse you over the destination or timing of your STM. Pray for God's perfect and pleasing will to be revealed.

Hearing God is sometimes only possible when you have taken, or are forced to take times of quietness, though we should all have a quiet time before God, when after our Bible reading and prayer, we stay quiet and focus on God and allow Him to speak to us. If you continually seek God's presence you will understand His will for your STM, the how (with whom), where and when. Prayer and abiding in the Father's will is essential for discerning what He wants to reveal to you (John 15:1-11, Acts 2:42 and 1 John 2:3-6). It is not just being able to hear God's voice that is important – so is obedience to Him and His Word! See James 1:22.

The Holy Spirit speaks lovingly, reassuringly and encourages. He will guide you into all truth (John 16:13), whilst the devil accuses, nags and speaks in a mocking manner. The devil will try to confuse you with regard to God's will for your STM by sowing doubt, fear and discouragement into your mind, "Has indeed God said?" (Genesis 3:1). After all, he does not want you to go, as you will be invading his territory!

Checks from God

- The Holy Spirit may forbid you (Acts 16:5-10 and Acts 19:10).
- Lack of opportunity, doors open or close (1 Corinthians 16:8-9, Colossians 4:3 and Revelation 3:8, but in 2 Corinthians 2:12-13), even though a door had opened for Paul in Troas, he had no peace.
- Lack of peace (Colossians 3:15), or lack of a direct word from God (a rhema word) (Psalm 119:105 and Isaiah 30:1-2, 21).
- If you have the mind of Christ then the correct fruit and attitude will be manifested within your spirit (1 Corinthians 2:16 and Galatians 5:22-23). Do you have joy or peace about a given decision or will? (Psalm 16:11, Isaiah 55:12, 2 Corinthians 5:7 and Philippians 4:7). Is there doubt or faith, love or fear, joy or unhappiness, patience or impatience?[1]

Chapter 9

Who Should Go

'As the eyes of servants look to the hand of their masters, as the eyes of a maid to the hand of her mistress, so our eyes look to the Lord our God...' (Psalm 123:2).

The person who picks and leads a team on a short-term mission (STM) has a lot more responsibilities, trials, problems and burdens than those who are part of the team. As the saying goes, 'the buck stops here,' and if you're the leader, then it stops with you! If you belong to a mission organization you should know what you're doing, but for a first time leader of a mission trip, it can be a daunting task.

Leading a mission team in one's own country is relatively easy, but being responsible abroad is quite another matter as the stakes get higher and problems can be more difficult to solve. In many different countries in Africa, I found out the mistake or fault may not have been mine, but the cost always was!

Who is an ideal candidate, who is a potential risk, who would I like to join the team, and what are the reasons for going on a STM?

Reasons for Going on a STM

There are many reasons why a person wants to be part (or does become a member) of a STM team but not all reasons and motives are honourable, whilst others are more understandable.

- God has called me.
- For the adventure or experience.
- Because I can afford it (because I can!).
- Want to be obedient to the Great Commission.
- Asked to join the team for the exposure to missions.
- Because my friend is going and I want to join her/him.
- Because I want to come for the ride (not that they say that), someone has offered to pay for them or the church is paying.
- Gap year – a break before studies begin, it looks good on the C.V./résumé or you have to do something over the next year and do not fancy getting a job at present.
- Trying to run away or avoid your responsibilities or duties.
- Time of trauma, heartbreak or tragedy and need to get away from familiar surroundings or bad memories etc.

Non-Christian Team Members

The Church in America is very big on STMs – especially humanitarian and development aid, building work, feeding the poor and medical help etc. which has led to a rise in allowing skilled non-Christians becoming part of the mission team. On occasions people of other faiths have gone along on some church mission trips (without realising the Christian content!), purely as humanitarian or development aid to use their skills, but this is just asking for trouble. The Bible warns: 'Do not be unequally yoked together with unbelievers. For what fellowship has righteousness with lawlessness? And what communion has light with darkness?' (2 Corinthians 6:14).

There may be exceptions to the rule – very few and far between, (a husband and wife as part of the church team). Only one spouse was converted after marriage and the other is not. An individual under consideration may be faithful, helpful and a good natured member of your church youth group, who is not a Christian (as yet) and it may be this mission which tips the balance, or it may be this mission that they begin to play up and upset the entire team or your host!

One danger with humanitarian aid is that the most essential and important tasks for which we exist (to glorify God, to share the Good News and to be a witness) can either be lost or crowded out.

Children, Youth and the Team Members

In recent years some churches have permitted children (as young as ten or eleven) to be part of a STM team if accompanied by a parent or relative. But is this wise? Whilst it could birth an interest in missions, it could be problematic. Who will look after your child when you are busy and what can a child of ten or eleven realistically contribute to the team?

Some teenagers are more mature than others. Some are quiet and shy, others are extroverts and some can be difficult. Many of us have had zeal without knowledge and we have all made mistakes in the past, so bear that in mind, before you decide to exclude (or decline) someone from joining the STM team.

Elderly and Team Members with Disabilities

There are some parts of the world where an elderly person may not be able to cope; in a cramped bus, or where you have to run for your seat or stand for five hours on public transport over potholed roads. This can be true of a team member with a disability who uses a wheelchair when much of the developing world has little to no wheelchair access, or the nearest hospital could be some distance away, and ill equipped at best. Facilities in some countries or districts are very poor with no health and safety considerations.

Warnings, Considerations and Payment

Beware of freeloaders and spongers – if the church is paying for the mission trip, you will get a lot more applicants than if each individual is responsible for raising their own finances. Some people only come for the "free holiday/vacation," whilst those who have not contributed have nothing to lose if they drop out, fly home early or fool around and are sent home. On the other hand, you do not want to limit the trip only to those who 'have' and decline the 'have-nots,' discriminating against those who do not have disposable income, who may not have a circle of friends or relatives that can help them is also wrong.

After announcing that a church is going on a STM, some have asked for an initial deposit as a refundable token payment, before the team has been picked. This separates the 'serious ones' from those who are 'just looking' because having half your 'proposed team' fall away after a month of preliminary meetings (to discuss the STM) is disheartening. Other leaders, discuss the STM, pick a team and then take a non-refundable deposit (e.g. £50 / $80) from each member.

Some applicants may be unable to attend different church meetings or outreaches because of essential prior commitments – family or job responsibilities and so should not be excluded from the team application due to an apparent lack of commitment.

Once you know who is going, then a period of payments needs to be worked out. A second non-refundable deposit, often to buy the plane tickets or to pay a deposit on the accommodation, is essential and then three to five instalments over the next 2-8 months. If you are the mission treasurer, keep a log of each payment received and issue receipts. A separate bank account should be opened for the mission money in the names of two unrelated people.

If you need a visa to enter a country, you may have to travel to the country's embassy and apply in person.

Release of Liability and Team Covenant

We live in an age where health and safety, coupled with risk assessment are at an all-time peak. Whilst all travel involves some measure of risk – you don't want to be sued by some zealous parent or individual who has had an accident on a STM whilst under your care or supervision. Search online for a 'Release of Liability' form or write a suitable and legal one yourself. This should be filled out by all participants, so that leader(s), the church or mission organization and all concerned will not be liable and cannot be sued if an accident occurs or anything unfortunate happens. These should be signed, dated and kept in a safe place. A duplicate copy should be given to each person who signed.

Each member of the STM team should sign a Team Covenant, a basic written agreement that each member will cooperate with the team leader and all the other members of the mission. To do their duties as unto the Lord, that they will be Christ-like, considerate towards others and stay clear of the use of improper language, coarse joking, discrimination, racism, tobacco, drugs, alcohol and improper sexual conduct.

The Team Covenant should be signed and dated in the presence of the leader and the other members of the team. Each member should receive a duplicate copy of the Covenant. The Team Covenant is something to fall back on if a team member begins to cause concern; the leader can pull out the Covenant and remind the person of their pledge/agreement.

Expectation and Realisation

For leaders: Sometimes expectation and realisation is interlinked with the preparation (or lack of it) long before you arrive at your STM destination. This is also coupled with what your host thinks you're going to do, what you have planned to do and whether or not this has been communicated clearly (leader to leader) and then passed onto your team.

As a leader have you asked your host what they want you to do? Has this been passed on to your team, so that they know what they will be doing? Have you spoken to your host over the phone, by email or video conferencing to clarify all points? Do you and your host know the skills, talents and giftings that are available amongst the team? Does the host need money in advance for a deposit to book accommodation or larger amounts to buy in supplies ready for your arrival? Does the leader need to meet with the host face-to-face and discuss any number of issues and to see the available facilities? The host might be quite comfortable in his or her accommodation, but a STM team might not be used to roughing it.

Is the host clear on who is coming, exact numbers, general ages and how many of each sex, including any married couples? You should try to keep STM-ers of a similar age and same sex in each room/dormitory, unless you need an older person for added security or because of their maturity. At other times, friends band together in groups and they do the job for you. Beware of someone being left out!

Chapter 10

The Dream Team

'He [Jesus] went up on the mountain and called to Him those that He Himself wanted...' (Mark 3:13).

If you are the leader who decides the team, then allow God to guide you to pick the dream team. Who you should invite (or take) and who should not be going; whether the trip should be open to all or selective ages (youth groups or 20-30s) to a limited number (4 to 12 persons etc.) or a larger group (20 to 40 persons). Remember that the larger the group the greater the logistics of plane seats, accommodation, transport, eating out, purchasing supplies in a small village for self-catering etc. Eating arrangements can be problematic for large groups, but generally not if you book in advance and do self-catering, even if only for breakfast and the evening meal. How many seats does the minibus or coach have? How many beds or room for camping mattresses/bed rolls does the hired hall or apartment have? Do not be a burden to your host.

As the team leader your job is to do the will of the Lord and by ignoring the small still voice of the Holy Spirit or obvious signs of someone's immaturity or lack of commitment, you are setting yourself up for trouble, disharmony within the team and a possible lack of blessing on the STM. Before you pick your team, you will need to know how much it will cost, or thereabouts and let prospective STM-ers know, the projected cost per person, or the correct amount.

If you go with a church or organization on your STM, then there is often a set number of places for practical reasons. At other times and especially for churches, they are happy to take along as many as can come, as long as each team member pays their own way and is committed to the work. Whilst a large team can do more work than just a handful, they can be difficult to manage, especially if there are a few who are prone to rebel and do not desire to pull their own weight. If working on a building site, e.g. constructing a church building or hospital, or boring a water hole, too many people will get in each other's way. There needs to be order and safety.

If you are applying to a mission organization to join their STM, then bear in mind that your application *may* be turned down. There is no automatic right of acceptance. Each mission has its own criteria and things that they look out for. You may be too young, too old, not in the best of health, not able enough or not have the correct skills. Your church leaders may not be able to financially support you, or feel that you have not shown enough commitment to the local fellowship. Prove yourself at home first, then abroad.

Picking the Team – The Options

- Open to anyone and everyone, of all ages from different churches or youth groups.
- Only for those within your church or youth or cell group.
- Selectively ask those with whom you would be happy to take along and be responsible for, especially if they are from your church or youth group.
- Prayerfully allow God to guide you as Jesus handpicked His disciples after a night of prayer and invite people.

Finances to Thought

Things to consider as to why I should go on a STM and not let fear get in the way.

- Finances – God will provide for all my needs.
- Faith – God is faithful.
- Fun – it will be fun and enjoyable working for the Lord as well as hard work!
- Fear – do not allow fear of the unknown to paralyze you.
- Thought – should I go, versus, do I want to go?

'...We also...do not cease to pray for you, and to ask that you may be filled with the knowledge of His will in all wisdom and spiritual understanding' (Colossians 1:9).

Problem People

- Members of your team who are uncommitted or half-hearted, and those with an unteachable spirit.
- Those who come with ulterior motives – especially if the financial liability or responsibility is not theirs.
- Those who have come to see the sights and to shop till they drop or treats the STM as a holiday/vacation.
- The isolationist who *only* wants to work alone.
- Those who think they are superior to others and look down on those to whom they have been sent *to serve*.
- Hygiene freaks, those who think they are allergic to anything and everything, and the hypochondriacs!
- The moaners and complainers, about anything and everything. The 'If I had done this' personality, I would have done it this way, which would have been much better!

- Those who choose not to have personal contact with the locals, they may even have a superior attitude.
- Those who think their STM ends when they leave their hosts' church or community and *refuse* to keep in contact when the hosts have been so kind, warm and considerate.

More Harm than Good

On any mission trip, an individual or an unprepared team can do more harm than good. Some negative and harmful traits as well as oversights are:

- Little to no preparation – not understanding the culture or lack of resources etc.
- No vaccinations or personal medical supplies.
- Refusal to interact with the locals.
- Selfishness – do it my way.
- Arrogance and critical – I know best and am the best.
- Pride and insensitive – superior attitude and I have all the answers, can't teach me anything.
- Flaunting your wealth – money, clothes and gadgets.
- Acting like a cash-cow – giving money and gifts to anyone who asks with no regard to consequences.
- Stubborn – we do it like this or not at all!
- Lack of communication – this is what they want (without asking the host church!).
- Leaving things undone – unfinished jobs, that which cannot be accomplished without further financial aid.
- Lack of foresight – if the water pump breaks, can the locals replace the parts? Do they have the money?
- Prayerlessness, and not reading and applying the truths of the Bible.

Jesus said to the disciples, "Let us go into the next towns, that I may preach there also, because for this purpose I have come forth" (Mark 1:38).

Leaders and the Team

Members of any STM team can greatly assist the leader by being submissive to them and taking their advice; whilst a great leader will know the strengths and weaknesses of their team. There is also the problem when older STM members refuse to submit to a younger leader. A leader should bring out the best in each member, and know (or discover) their qualities and strengths and utilise them. If your STM consists of development aid where specialist skills (or giftings) are needed, *do not assume* the builder wants to build, the chef wants to cook, the bus driver wants to drive the hired mini-bus. The gravedigger may not want to dig ditches to lay water pipes or the teacher may not want to supervise the teenagers. Ask them.

Valid Passport and Visa

If you do not have a passport then you had better get one soon! They cost money and take time to process. For those who already have a passport, make sure that it will not expire whilst you are on your STM. Are there enough blank pages for Immigration and Departure stamps, and visa(s)? Some countries will expect you to have at least six months outstanding on your passport (sometimes a year) before they even allow you to enter their country or before they will issue you with a visa.

Visa requirements change from one nationality to the next as do their costs. If you join a mission organization, they will advise you on the type of visa needed and how to apply. You may have to travel to the country's embassy to get a visa in person. Some companies offer a visa processing service, where you post/ship your passport and completed application to them. Some embassies want to know not only your job, but that of your parents and grandparents! Some embassies want to see a letter from your consular, for a British citizen, this costs £45 ($72)!

Some embassies insist on a letter of invite before they will issue you with a visa. You can obtain one (via email) from a tour company, a hotel, an individual residing within the country or a company or organization. Some hotels or guest houses will send you a letter of invite if you make a reservation with them, as will tour companies, when you make a booking with them; some government approved tourist companies will send you one for a fee (around $25). Some hotels will only send a letter (via email) *if* you make a reservation for three days, whilst others are not so stringent. Just email and ask for a letter of invite. Also see chapter 11, Concerns and Visas.

Parents, Guardians, Siblings Etc.

Not every parent, guardian, sibling or spouse is thrilled with the prospect of the one they love, going away on a STM, taking a year out, or being away from them for two weeks or more. There may be concerns, including financial, emotional and safety issues. Abraham may have been pestered and perhaps even cross-examined by his family when God called him to go on his mission, leaving as men would say, 'a certain for an uncertain good.' I am sure his friends told him it would be foolish to leave behind the good pastures, familiar surroundings and the warm home life. Undoubtedly they told him not to heed his wild imaginations of the call of God. Thankfully, he was obedient to the call of God and embarked on a mission that not only changed his life, but the course of history and in him all the families of the earth have been blessed.

Logistics – an Essential Role
Within a large STM team, there needs to be someone in charge of the logistics which is the practical preparation of: transportation, accommodation, how to feed the team (self-catering or eating out), purchasing supplies/materials for projects etc. This is often the team leader's responsibility, the host or shared responsibility, but some duties are delegated to responsible or veteran members of the team.

Sometimes logistic leaders are largely stuck at base camp, especially if you are cooking for a large team, while the team goes off and evangelises or does humanitarian work. From day-to-day, two members of the team may have to remain at base camp (on a rotational basis) to assist the logistics member or host member. Their work is no less important than the ones on the "front line" as each member has his or her duty to do. If a regiment was not fed and supplied then it would fail in its mission. Those at base camp may be cooking, doing the laundry, chauffeuring, buying supplies, confirming the meetings and perform many other duties and double-check all details. Also see chapter 30, Working with the Locals.

Be Prepared
We all have gifts and talents and on your STM they can come to the fore and be a blessing to many, whilst love is a universal language. Long before your STM commences make sure you are prepared:

- Spiritually – am I a real Christian, truly converted/saved, and a disciple of the Lord Jesus Christ? Do I read my Bible and pray daily? Am I faithful in attending church meetings and do I participate? Do I desire to share the Good News with others?
- Physically – do I have health problems or a medical condition, which may exacerbate on the STM or endanger my own life? Am I unhealthy, over or under weight? Am I addicted to junk food or dependant on my fix of coffee, chocolate, medicine, cigarettes or alcohol? If you have issues with the last two then it is best that you get them dealt with before you join a STM team.
- Mentality – do I know why I want to go and why I should go? What is expected of me? Do I realise it is not a holiday/vacation and I will encounter some discomforts. There will be difficulties as I may be working with a group who are unknown to me, and stresses and strains are inevitable with possible personality clashes.

Chapter 11

Concerns and Visas

After Jesus' resurrection, He appeared to the disciples and said, "Peace to you! As the Father has sent Me, I also send you" (John 20:21).

There are many dangers involved in short-term missions (STMs), as there is a danger in doing anything, in any place, at any time. The person who decides to stay at home to be safe has forgotten about earthquakes, typhoons, hurricanes, terrorist attacks, toxic spills, fires, floods and many other dangers. We should not allow fear of "what might happen" to paralyze us to inaction, but we all need to be wise.

Since the Arab Spring, which began in December 2010 in Tunisia, North Africa, much of North Africa and the Middle East has undergone dramatic change and seen much turmoil in the past six years. With the rise of the Islamic State (IS) (also known as ISIS, ISIL, Daesh and Daish) in 2014, sweeping into and taking control over large swathes of Iraq, Syria and other parts of the Middle East; with affiliated groups in pockets in North Africa and northern Nigeria etc., multitudes of Christians, (plus Muslims, minority groups, including aid workers) have been taken hostage and endured torture, rape, mutilations etc.; many are killed, including women, children and babies. Many young women have been forced to renounce the Christian faith (or those of other faiths) to embrace Islam and are sold as sex-slaves or as brides for jihadists. The ransoming of Christian hostages in parts of Iraq is rife. These are the countries that you should avoid on your STM. Terrorist attacks have also been against tourists/foreigners in Tunisia, Egypt and Mali in West Africa. In November 2015, 130 people were killed in Paris, France, and around 300 were injured in simultaneous terrorist attacks. These included gunmen/women and suicide bombers. Islamic terrorists have also struck in many other countries from Pakistan to Indonesia.

Many governments of the world issue travel warnings to its citizens, places to avoid because of civil, political or other forms of unrest; as well as dangers because of terrorist activity and recent natural disasters. Some countries that are listed as dangerous are quite safe apart from isolated areas or certain regions in which the local government may have no control. After the attacks in Paris in November 2015, the American government issued a worldwide travel alert to its citizens.

From time to time, there are outbreaks of diseases, fears of epidemics, scare-mongering, actual epidemics (e.g. SARS, Ebola, Zika virus etc.) and occasional pandemics. Other preventable diseases such as Cholera, TB, Yellow Fever, Chicken Pox, Measles, Mumps etc. do break-out in parts of the world, though some in isolated towns or districts. These can cause myriads of deaths amongst those who are too poor to aid preventions by inoculation, immunisation or vaccination.

It would be very unwise and foolish to go on a STM to an infected area (e.g. Ebola) and expose your team to life-altering consequences – that is unless you are the medical team! Sometimes these hot spots of infection only last a few months or can continue for years, whilst at other times, the whole scenario can rapidly change and a town, which could be in a state of "lock-down," can be open for business as usual within weeks.

Natural disasters can occur at any time. Being a Christian on a STM does not make you or your team untouchable or immune from disasters and dangers. Every mission team leader would be wise to consider having an emergency evacuation plan for the team (or a team member), not only for medical emergencies, but in cases of terrorism and natural disasters etc. In mid-April 2010, a volcano erupted in Iceland and volcanic ash closed the airspace over parts of Europe for six days. Thousands of flights (in and out of Europe) were grounded. This stranded 100,000+ passengers across the globe, on both sides of the Atlantic and the Middle East. Some insurance policies have 'Industrial Action' and 'Volcanic Disruption' options. Finding out what your travel insurance covers (before you purchase it) and what it DOES NOT COVER is essential. 'Acts of God' are an exemption clause where you are not covered!

Valid Passport and Visa

Do you have a valid passport and do you need a visa? If you join a mission organization, they will advise you on the type of visa needed and what you should fill in under 'nature of your visit.' Visas can be Single Entry, Multiple Entry/Multi-Entry, Business/Work or Tourist. A Single Entry visa is often the cheapest and a Business visa the most expensive. With most countries, you can apply for your visa from your home country, some you get on arrival at the country of destination. If you are already in another country you may be able to apply for a visa from that country. In Asia, some travel businesses will do the leg work for you and take your paperwork and passport to the embassy and bring it back. In your home country you may be able to pay a visa processing company to do this on your behalf via the postal service. This works well if you need two or more visas from different embassies. Some visas are time sensitive, they begin on the day of issue and count down, from weeks to months. Forward planning is essential.

Some embassies are *only* open on certain days at certain times, and they frequently have long queues, so arrive early. Check that the correct visa has been issued to you and in your name. Some visas have been stuck in the passport of another person! Many years ago, to apply for a visa to India, I had to give my flight details and my ticket number. That is, I had to buy my plane ticket *before* I could receive permission to enter the country!

Some countries permit a transit visa for x amount of days when you are just passing through. The Russian embassy in Mongolia issues them for ten days if you are using the Trans-Siberian Railway from Ulaanbaatar, Mongolia to Moscow, Russia, which takes five days and four nights. On a transit visa, hotels in Moscow only allow you to stay two nights. If your plane does not depart until the third or fourth day, check-out after two days and check-in to a new hotel.

If you are an independent STM-er then it is advisable NOT to tick the Business or Work visa box. Whilst you are participating in your "Father's business," to use Jesus' words, you are not going as a businessperson to make money, to buy or sell or to trade in wares and so the Tourist, Visitor or Pleasure box can be ticked. Under the nature of your visit, it is advisable NOT to write 'missionary' or 'preacher of the Good News' (and who is to say you will preach anyway?), as you may be turned back at the airport or border and refused entry – even if you write humanitarian or development work.

With most countries, you will have to fill out an Arrivals Card and these are issued on the plane or at Immigration. Sometimes you have to return your half of the Arrivals Card on your departure, so don't lose it! Be cautious of who you speak to at the airport or aboard the plane, don't go revealing the mission secrets to strangers. (This is the same with social media). They may not agree with the work, and if a national, could report you at Immigration.

You can get visa extensions whilst inside a country (subject to the issuing staff, the embassies policies and your nationality) or often it is a case of leaving the country (which can be a simple land or sea border) and re-entering on the same day (like Thailand to Myanmar and back), or within a few days or weeks. The embassy, your host (or an up-to-date travel guidebook) can advise on this. Policies can change without prior notice. In China in 2011, we had to book into a "government approved hotel" before we could extend our visa.

Chapter 12

Money for your Mission

'And God is able to make all grace abound towards you, that you, always having all sufficiency in all things, may have an abundance for every good work' (2 Corinthians 9:8).

There are many ways and methods of raising support and obtaining your financial needs for your short-term mission (STM); some of which you may feel led to do, some of which you may feel prompted not to do and some of which you may disdain. What is right for one person may not be right for others, and if you are an older person going on a STM there are some options, which a younger person would not hesitate to do, which are not fitting for an older person. There are many and varied views in regards to raising support and financing STMs with good arguments for and against some of these methods. I will give the options and it is for you to be led from God for how *you* should finance your STM. However, DO NOT GO INTO DEBT, by taking out a loan, putting it on the credit card, charge card or borrowing, as this is not an option to finance your STM.

Financial Options
1. Use money from your savings account. However, paying for a STM in its *entirety* from your savings can hinder others from being a financial blessing towards the mission.
2. Ask your church to assist you. For some, asking a church to *entirely* finance their mission is unethical, if they support the church little and/or are well-off themselves.
3. Ask your parents/family for a contribution. They may not be impressed by your decision to go on a STM or could greatly surprise you by their delight that you are doing something you believe in. They may be glad to see the back of you for a few weeks or months! Some people have asked their employer for financial help or items for humanitarian work.
4. Praying to God to move people to send you money. You can either keep quiet and tell only God your needs or pray and inform others at the same time.
5. Carry out various sponsored events to help raise support – sponsored walk, cycle ride or swimming etc.
6. Make items to sell, baking cakes, bread or bird boxes etc.

7. Sell items you own – your car, sports equipment, jewellery, computer games, books etc. Some items greatly depreciate in value over time, so if you intend to replace an item after your STM then perhaps you should not sell it in the first place.
8. Get a part-time job or do some overtime/extra hours.
9. Offer your services to clean cars, dig the garden, sweep the yard or baby-sit etc.
10. Speak to your youth leader, pastor or head of missions within your church and see how they can help.
11. Any combination of the above, though you should always try to get your local church onboard, as you are part of the local family of God and your endeavours can stir others to be obedient to the Great Commission and raise prayer support.

Whatever you feel led to do, wrap it up in much prayer, ask God's blessing on the endeavour and do it with all your might as unto the Lord.

The Church and Finances

If your local church sends you out on a STM then it is generally their responsibility to pay for the mission, though not all churches have the resources (Romans 10:15 and 1 Timothy 5:8, 18). The apostle Paul received money from some churches in order to minister to others because he did not want to be a financial burden (2 Corinthians 11:7-9 and 2 Thessalonians 3:8) – so don't be a burden to your local church! However, many churches would be delighted to assist any of their *committed* members to go on a STM; those who have proved faithful at home. In addition, if you have not put money into the pot (tithes and offerings) should the church take money out of the pot and support you?

The Philippian Church sent aid for Paul's necessities by the hand of Epaphroditus (Philippians 4:15-16) which was 'a sweet smelling aroma, an acceptable sacrifice, well pleasing to God.' On occasions, Paul asked various churches to 'help him on his way' or 'send him on his journey' (Romans 15:24, 1 Corinthians 16:6 and 2 Corinthians 1:15-16). Paul also asked the church to assist other fellow labourers (Romans 16:1-2 and 1 Corinthians 16:10-11).

If you have been a receiver of spiritual things, it is your duty to help minister in material things, to continue the spread of the Good News (Romans 15:26-29, 2 Timothy 1:16-18 and 3 John 5-8). If you have more than enough, it is your duty to share (Luke 3:8-11 and 1 John 3:17-18). The disciples sent aid to the brethren living in Judea (Acts 11:29-30 and Romans 15:26-28). The phrase, 'Send them forward on their journey' (3 John 6) means to provide aid for travelling preachers. These helps can be: accommodation, recommendations, food and money etc., whilst inhospitality is condemned (3 John 9-11). We can all help in our own little way.

Not Asking for Money

Most people who go on STMs are happy to ask people for their financial support, but this may not be you. Some may not feel able to ask for money towards their STM or like Abraham after rescuing Lot, he refused the spoils of war from the King of Sodom, thus not allowing the king any opportunity to boast that he had made Abraham rich (Genesis 14:12-24). You'll be surprised how many individuals or churches give small amounts towards STMs (or nothing at all) and then boast as if they entirely supported the mission team!

You may wish to make your needs known only to God or you may feel at liberty to share your prayer needs with a faithful friend, so that he or she can pray specifically and intelligently. Beware, they may feel that you are dropping hints; this can also be true of prayer: letters, emails and social media plugs. Only God knows the heart and the motives, but we can so easily deceive ourselves; do not despise gifts from family or friends or the widow's mite.

Whilst some people do not feel comfortable to ask for money for their STM they may wish to ask for financial support for supplies, such as for the construction of a building, a water pump, medical supplies, Bibles or other Christian materials. But, whatever they decide, it is between them and God. At other times, there may be no other option, but to look to God to supply all your money for your STM as all other avenues have failed.

Jesus said, "Seek first the Kingdom of God and His righteousness, and all these things shall be added unto you" (Matthew 6:33).

Your Own Provision

You may be praying for money for your STM and you may be the answer to your own needs! The apostle Paul worked as a tentmaker for a time (Acts 18:1-3 and 2 Thessalonians 3:7-9) which allowed him to pay his way whilst participating in the Great Commission. The term 'tentmaker' is now synonymous with Christians who work on the mission field to support themselves and/or who have an occupation, which permits them to stay within a country. Paul tried to provide for his own necessities and for those that were with him (Acts 20:34-35). If your church is hard-up and you are not, don't expect them to pay for your STM. Could you get yourself a Saturday job or extra hours? Work hard and save as much as you can towards the cost of your STM. It is wrong to expect others to make sacrifices to send you on your STM, if you have wasted you own resources on 'good living.'

Looking to God By Faith

God may call you to look to Him by faith for your needs (Hebrews 11:1) and if He has, you need to be guided by Him meticulously (see Psalm 32:8, Psalm 123:2, Proverbs 16:3 and Proverbs 16:9). Don't play with sin because sin separates us from God and God has said, "No good thing will He withhold from them that walk uprightly" (Psalm 84:11). Are you upright before God?

- Ask God (Matthew 7:7-8).
- Is it God's will? (1 John 5:14).
- Ask in Jesus' name, so that God will be glorified (John 14:13-14).
- Pray in faith and with faith, believing that you will receive (Mark 11:24).
- If you have sin in your heart your prayers will not be heard (Psalm 66:18).

The psalmist wrote: 'Unless the Lord builds the house, they labour in vain who build it...' (Psalm 127:1).

God's Provision and Trust God

We may tend to believe that God's provision will come by means of a stranger handing us large sums of money. Don't be disappointed if your parents, church, friends or work colleagues give you money towards your STM – this is God's provision. To scorn them as donors is to scorn God's means of support. God is practical! Be thankful for the widow's mite as well as the businessman's bonus!

Whatever you do, trust God to lead and guide you as He has promised to provide for your needs as long as we seek His Kingdom first (Matthew 6:33 and Philippians 4:19). We are also informed: 'Be anxious for nothing, but in everything by prayer and supplication, with thanksgiving, let your requests be made known to God and the peace of God, which surpasses all understanding will guard your hearts and minds through Christ Jesus' (Philippians 4:6-7). In the parable of the labourers, Jesus said, "You also go into the vineyard and whatever is right I will give you" (Matthew 20:4). Be encouraged!

J. Hudson Taylor, founder of the China Inland Mission said, "God's work, done God's way, will not lack God's resources."

Chapter 13

The Cost of the STM – your Budget

'Nor was there anyone among them who lacked; for all who were possessors of lands or houses sold them, and brought the proceeds of the things that were sold and laid them at the apostles' feet and they distributed to each as anyone had need' (Acts 4:34-35).

On any short-term mission (STM) there are lots of things to budget for and you do not want to cut corners or make a financial mistake as it will cost you in more ways than one. For those who are joining a mission organization, all the costs will have been worked out and they will be able to inform you of any other money you may need, or what is not included in the price. If you have a Student Card you may be able to get a discount on your plane ticket or other items.

If you are travelling with your church, (you may be the leader who is organising the trip) or a group of friends are making up the mission team, then the smaller your budget, the more strains and tensions that will arise. If your daily budget is tight, you may find yourself haggling over pennies and cents; a fraction of the cost of a chocolate/candy bar – and in that situation you lose sight of the purpose of the mission.

If you are an independent STM (you and a friend or a small team) and your budget is slim, if you get financially exploited, then it may take weeks to recover from your loss or overspend in the only overpriced hotel in town. Some towns are more expensive than others and whilst you may overspend in one place, you can make savings in others, assuming you move locations. Accommodation on the outskirts of a town is frequently cheaper than in the centre.

An extra £4 ($6.40) per person a day in a developing country can make all the difference between a flee pit of a room and one that is adequate, (based on two people sharing a room), whilst in Europe, the difference between adequate and nice can be an additional £25 ($40) per person (depending on location). Your church may have arranged your stay with the locals and whilst they may not charge you rent, you cannot be a burden to them, financially or otherwise.

If you are the leader of a young inexperienced STM team then you don't want to be taking them to flee pit accommodation! If you are fixed in a single location, renting an apartment for two weeks, a month or longer may be a better fiscal proposition, with amenities to cook the team's meals. If you are based in one location for weeks or months, then it is easier to work out the cost of living. If you will be in several locations, even across countries you will need to take an average costing of the entire trip.

Daily Living Expenses – Cost per Day

If you are going on your STM independently of a mission organization, or planning the trip for your church or friends you will need to work out your daily living expenses, the cost per day. This must include: accommodation, food and transport. As you will be going in pairs (or more) you must include your budget and the other STM-er's budget to get the total daily budget. For living expenses, if the cost per day is £24 ($38) for two people, this means a personal budget of £12 ($19) per day – this includes accommodation, travel and food. £12 ($19) per person per day (going in pairs) might be OK for South-East Asia, but in parts of Africa would be a stretch and would be nigh impossible in some African countries, such as Zambia or South Africa, where £18+ ($29+) per day is more realistic.

If you are doing a lot of travel inside a country then you may need to increase your budget to accommodate the extra miles of travel on public transport or fuel for the hired bus.

A larger budget per person may be needed for a group, unless you are renting an apartment or a complex. One STM team of fifteen people rented a house in Brazil with a swimming pool for two weeks and it was considerably cheaper than staying in a hotel. Youth hostels can be cheap, however, in China, you can get better facilities and at a lower cost in many hotels! In a hotel it is cheaper for two people to share the same room than if you had two single rooms. Some rooms can accommodate four or more people and therefore you pay less than if you had two rooms, though with less privacy and space. Most rooms are only used for half a day (at night) because in the daytime you will be outside doing the work of the Lord.

You should be eating together at the same restaurant, fast-food outlet or roadside food stall, so a common pot with all things shared is the easiest financial solution. However, disagreements can arise if your friend eats twice as much as you or only buys the expensive meals or branded fizzy drinks instead of the cheaper local ones. For a church mission team, each member should be allocated some personal money per week so that they can buy a drink or a snack when they want to. Otherwise the leader or the treasurer may be pestered every ten minutes, by thirsty or hungry youth. For STM teams who are not self-catering, it is best to set a value for each meal. Each STM-er can order what they want to that value. If their meal is more expensive, they then pay the extra. If it is under, they do not pocket the difference.

You can live and eat as cheap as you want to, but cockroach and rat infested hostels and rooms will get you down after a while, and can be damaging to your health. It is a false economy and can dampen your mood, making your STM less effective. Large teams cannot cope with poor accommodation. A mixed team of eight to ten people will need better accommodation and better food than just two people participating on their own STM who are more happy to go with the flow. Within any large group, there will be greater needs (the higher probability of more particular people) and by budgeting in additional finances it will make it easier for the group and hopefully, reduce the chances of illness, bedbug bites and grumblers!

Once a daily budget has been worked out, it needs to be double and triple-checked. You cannot afford to make a mistake. Then you need to add the plane ticket, visa (if needed), travel insurance (individually or as a team), any materials you may be taking with you and money for interpreters, love gifts etc. Members of your team may need inoculation, jabs and medication (anti-malarial tablets). As a team, you may be able to negotiate a group rate with you local doctor or health clinic. You should always add ten percent on top of your total budget (some churches will float this money to the team). This is 'emergency' or 'unforeseen circumstances' money, that if not used can be returned to the members (or church) when they arrive home.

Your Plane Ticket

The plane ticket is often the heftiest part of any STM budget unless you are flying on a budget airline, the no frills airlines.

Look to see what time your proposed flight departs and arrives before you purchase. It may depart at 10am in the morning, but can you drive the three hours to the airport (or catch the coach) and arrive within the two-hour check-in period, which means you will have to leave your home by 5am? Some evening flights mean that you arrive in the dark and will have to check straight into a hotel. It can take up to 1 hour for baggage reclaim and then you have to take public transport (but often a taxi) to your destination. Night-time taxis have a higher rate than day-time ones. If your proposed plane's return flight arrives late in the evening, will you be able to get a train or coach back home or be stuck at the airport until morning?

Shop around for plane tickets, as there are bargains to be had, search on the internet or negotiate a group deal with an airline or through a travel agent/broker. Midweek flights are generally cheaper (Tuesday-Thursday) than at weekends as are those that depart or arrive at odd times of the day or night. During holiday/vacation and festivals (peak season) prices increase and will decrease during low season or as supply and demand dictates. Weekend flights are more expensive as is Friday and Monday. International air passenger duty (departure taxes) can be high. Fuel duty can add an extra cost to your ticket even after you have bought it! If you use your credit card then a handling fee is often applied or a percentage of the ticket cost.

Some countries do not like permitting people into their country if they only have a one-way ticket. They are suspicious and think you may be a burden on their society or are up to no good. Make sure that the correct spelling of your name in on the ticket and keep the return/roundtrip ticket safe! Confirm the time of your departure three days in advance and remind the entire team!

Do not forget the cost of your travel to and from the airport. This may be by train, coach (minibus for a group) or by car and if it's the latter, you will need to budget the additional cost of a long stay car park (parking lot) if you're going for less than three weeks. Long stay car parks (parking lots) are always cheaper offsite in locked compounds than at the airport.

Visa Information

Visas – prices vary between countries and for different nationalities. Most consulates charge in U.S. dollars; the standard visa fee ranges from being free to around $200 (£125), though most are around $50 (£31) for a single entry visa. Multi-entry visas can cost considerably more and your visa may state by which method you can enter or exit the country – by land or by air, or state at which entry or exit. Unless your mission organization states otherwise you do not need a Business or Work visa (but a tourist one) as you are not going to trade, to make money. The cost of a visa can change from one month to the next, depending on diplomatic relationships and how hard-up the country is! In Asia and Africa, you *only* pay in U.S. dollars.

Inoculations and Jabs

Prevention is better than cure so have all the jabs and inoculations you need before you depart. If you are ill, have a disease or health problem (physical or mental), you should contact a doctor/physician to seek professional medical help before departing on your STM. The author is not a doctor/physician or counsellor. The related medical contents of this book cannot take the place of advice from a medical professional, and is not intended to, but is included as an aid and a guide. Tetanus and Hepatitis jabs are free in the UK – see your local doctor. Prices do vary between health centres for other non-NHS jabs, and only designated centres can give certain inoculations such as Yellow Fever. You must always take the accompanying Yellow Fever Certificate with you when you travel abroad as the border guards/Immigration may ask to see it. Without it, you will not be permitted to enter certain countries or be issued with a visa! Keep it with your passport.

Jabs x3 against the rabies virus are expensive, around £120 ($192), but is advisable if you are going into remote jungle-like areas or if you know you will be around animals/bats within a rabies infected areas. If you are bitten or scratched by an infected creature you will need another course of treatment, ideally within 24hrs which is equally expensive, but potentially life saving.

Medication

Some anti-malarial tablets are taken daily, others are taken weekly and you may have to take them two weeks (or longer) before departure and two weeks after your return. There can be side effects; but you DO NOT want to catch malaria. It is reported that fifty percent of local medicines (especially anti-malarial brands) in some developing countries are ineffective. Expect to pay around £50-100 ($80-160) for a six-month supply in a Western nation, plus the cost of a private prescription.

If you are on the pill, some medicines can make this form of contraception less effective, so married couples beware; on your one year STM you may return home with an extra mouth to feed!

A Cholera vaccination is two sachets of powder and two containers of medicine, which are mixed with water and taken within 6 weeks of each other, £33 ($53). Can be free on the NHS.

Tick-borne encephalitis is three vaccines, two before you depart (one month apart) and one after 12 months costs around £132 ($211).

To combat the affects of altitude sickness your doctor can prescribe DIAMOX (Acetazolamide) around £8 ($12.80) for 28 tablets, a two-week supply (two a day).

Travel Insurance

Travel Insurance is from £50-200 ($80-320) for three months to a year, depending on age and any previous health issues. You will probably have to get a backpackers/gap year type travel insurance as the majority of insurance companies do not extend cover for lengthy periods of time. If you're only doing your STM in one country it should be cheaper than if you will be passing through several. If you are part of a mission organization they will be able to advise you.

I do not advise travelling abroad on a STM without travel insurance and be very diligent in filling out the application form. Always put in the correct details, otherwise your cover may not be valid.

Shop around online for good insurance deals and remember that if you participate in extreme sports e.g. bungee jumping, cliff jumping or jet skiing, on your day off, you may not be covered. These should be avoided on STMs, as King Solomon said, "Do not be overly wicked, nor be foolish, why should you die before your time?" (Ecclesiastes 7:17).

'Acts of God' are not covered and this can include volcanic ash shutting down entire flight paths over many countries. Some airlines by law are responsible for their stranded passengers and 'reasonable compensation' can be claimed, e.g. hotel bill. Always read the small print (however tedious) and remember that most policies do not cover expensive electrical goods, laptops, digital cameras and only a limited amount of cash. Always keep the details of your travel insurance emergency telephone number and policy details handy. In some countries, you can have two broken legs and be lying in a hospital corridor, but you will not be treated unless you have the means to pay!

For European citizens, the free European Health Insurance Card (EHIC) entitles you to reduced costs (or sometimes free) healthcare and treatment within the European economic area and Switzerland. It is NOT a substitute for travel insurance.

What to Budget For
The prices below are a general guide.

- Plane ticket and travel to and from the airport, plus taxes if not included in the cost of the plane ticket.
- Visa – prices vary between countries, from nothing to $200 (£125), though most are around $50 (£31).
- Inoculations and jabs – within the UK many are free; others range from £40-60 ($60-100). Jabs x3 against the rabies virus are around £120 ($192), and need to be repeated if you get bitten by a rabies carrier. (I've never had a rabies jab).
- Medication – anti-malarial tablets from £50-100 ($80-160) for a six-month supply, plus a private prescription.
- Travel Insurance from £50-200 ($80-320) for three months to a year. Prices vary between companies.
- Cost per day – which must include accommodation, food and transport.
- Emergency money – 10% extra on top of your calculated total.
- Gift money to help others and to bless them.
- Money for interpreters, guides, vehicle hire, local evangelist, pastor etc.
- Bibles, gospels, booklets, tracts etc. Tools and materials for any humanitarian aid and gifts for your host etc.

Chapter 14

How to Travel with Money

'Owe no one anything, except to love one another' (Romans 13:8).

Nobody wants to be robbed of their possessions or be stuck abroad on their short-term mission (STM) with no money. This chapter covers the methods of travelling with money; using ATMs (cash points), hard cash and other financial options. An independent STM may have additional financial concerns, which an organized mission would not. If you are going on a mission across many nations for a lengthy period of time, then a selection of financial options are the best; hard cash and cash cards, so that if one option fails or is limited in one area, there is another method to fall back on.

I have always travelled with hard cash (American dollars and British pound sterling, though euros are also good), alongside cash cards and credit cards. Travelling with lots of money is all well and good, unless you get robbed! Wear a money belt under your clothes. I do not recommend the following two methods, but they may be great for you.

Traveller's Cheques and Prepaid Card

Traveller's cheques have a high rate of commission and in some developing countries, they are not widely accepted or *only* certain brands can be cashed.

With a prepaid Travel Money Card (TMC), the Financial Services Compensation Scheme does not always apply; there are many restrictions on its use, and generally higher fees than a cash point transaction. I have never used this.

A Visa Prepaid CitizenCard (which you apply and buy) doubles as proof of identity and age. The minimum age is twelve. A fee of from 0-3% is taken from the amount of money put on the card (a load up) and a fee can be incurred when you withdraw money. I have never used this.

Mobile Banking and Cash Points/ATMs

Some people prefer mobile/cell banking and pay their bills by means of a phone transfer or via an App on their smartphone. In one East African country, many of its citizens use their mobiles/cell phones (not smartphones) to send and receive money, and to pay for smaller purchases. I have never used this. A number of companies like PayPal and Apple Pay also work via your laptop, Tablet, smartphone or iPhone.

Most capitals of the world have Automatic Teller Machines (ATMs), commonly referred to as cash points. Cash cards/debit cards are a great fiscal blessing to STM-ers or travellers. As the years tick by, cash points that accept VISA or MasterCard continue to grow and are located in more and more towns and even obscure villages. However, in some districts or countries, one or the other is not widely used, though in my experience, VISA is more widely accepted. If you are going to stay in a particular city abroad, search online to see if there are ATMs that will accept your cash card.

Most financial institutions charge for cash withdrawals abroad when using their VISA or MasterCard debit card. This is generally a set fee of £1 ($1.60) or more, plus 2-5% of the transaction amount. The bank ATM from which you withdraw may also charge a fee. Take out the maximum amount in each transaction rather than use the ATM twice a week.

It is important that you inform your bank/building society and credit card provider that you will be using your cards abroad. Ask them to make a note on their records, as transactions out of the ordinary may be deemed as fraudulent and your card may be cancelled or swallowed by the ATM and you will not get it back! Also, make sure that your card will not expire when you are on your STM. Getting a new card shipped out by courier is expensive.

Find out online or use a guidebook to discover if there are any cash points outside of the capital (or major cities). Make sure you take enough money to last you to the next cash point or beyond.

Credit Cards and American Dollars

Credit cards should be used responsibly and not to incur debt. If you are not paying your balance off IN FULL every month then you should not be using them (the same with a charge card). On the mission field, I use them to buy plane tickets and hire vehicles and they also carry your insurance excess if you have an accident. I have known people to go on holiday/vacation and become incredibly ill and hospitalised. They have had to use their credit card to pay their hospital bill which was later reimbursed by their travel insurance.

You can withdraw money from cash points using your credit card (a Cash Advance) but I do not recommend it. You will get charged daily interest at a high rate, and some cards also charge a transaction fee or a non-sterling/dollar fee. Some businesses add a handling fee when you pay by credit card. Credit cards may be swiped through the machine twice (thus charging you twice). You may not realise this until you have checked your statement at home and weeks or months could have elapsed! If you bank online, be cautious when using the internet abroad. You can ask a family member to open your mail and check your monthly statements.

The American dollar is a strong currency; it is stable and is widely used across the world. In many countries in South-East Asia (e.g. Cambodia, Vietnam), you can pay for your purchases (even at some restaurants) in dollars, whilst some establishments prefer it. Most embassies will expect you to pay for their visa in American dollars and you have to pay airport taxes in developing countries (in dollars) if this tax was not included in the price of your plane ticket.

I have never had denomination (bills) of higher than $50 and have travelled with mostly $20 bills. In South-East Asia, they are very keen on $1 bills and as with most foreign notes, they have to be clean and crisp. If they are marked or creased some Foreign Exchange Bureaux (FEB) or shops will not accept them. Smaller denominations of $1, $5 and $10 also occur a lesser exchange rate than larger bills. Always take a combination of bills and keep them in a waterproof money belt hidden under your clothes.

In the fourth week of January 2009, the American dollar to British pound sterling rate changed to $1.35 to the £1.00 (a 23-year low), rebounding a week later to $1.39. If a person in Britain exchanged £1,000 (as compared to November 2008 rate, which was $2.00 to £1.00), they would have lost $650 (£406) worth of purchasing power.

Foreign Exchange Bureaux

Be very careful when exchanging money, not only at a Foreign Exchange Bureaux (FEB), but *especially* at border crossings. At border crossings there are often a number of people on the street exchanging money. More often than not, they will approach you. Haggle for the best rate between the workers. Make sure you do the exchange rate calculations on your own calculator as some may be fixed and not in your favour! Looking at new money can be confusing. Take your time and count the money out, do not be hassled or rushed and check each note/bill that it is the correct denomination with the right amount of zeros on it.

With FEBs, beware of a commission rate which is deducted from your money. This can make the good exchange rate not so good as money is creamed of the top and into their pocket, not yours! Always ask for mixed denominations as a wad of pre-counted money in single bills may lack one or two notes. Look confident as you examine the notes, as if you know what you are doing! It is always helpful to look on the internet to see what the country's bills look like as you do not want to be handed worthless out-of-circulation notes.

Whilst exchange rates vary by the minute, check online to see the general exchange rate and try to get the best rate.

Most major currencies can be purchased within your own country, but where and when you buy it, can vary greatly. Research has shown that it does depend on picking the right place and the right time, though the latter is not so easy to 'predict' but research in the former is easier – shop around for the best deal! In the UK, you can often get a better rate if you exchange £500+ ($800). Differences between rates can seem deceptively slim, but if it is not in your favour, it can quickly push up the cost of your STM! The person who exchanges at the 'last minute' at the airport or an international train station will get the worst rate. Beware of commission!

Receiving Money

If you are abroad and you need money quickly you can use Money Gram or Western Union, the latter having more branches where money can be sent and received. An instant transfer costs around £25 ($40), but if you can wait a day or two the service costs around £10 ($16).

You can also transfer money from one bank or building society account to one abroad. If the sending and receiving banks are of the same company then it is generally a free service, but sending money between different banks can costs upwards of £20 ($32) and can take up to one week. The receiving bank may charge for their service and exchange rates (which fluctuate) can drop significantly within a week. A family member at home could deposit some money into your bank account, which you withdraw via your debit card.

I have read in some travel books that people who are really hard up can sell their blood to hospitals or clinics. I cannot recommend this. If there is poor hygiene you could end up catching a disease from a second-hand un-sterilised syringe etc.

Good planning is the best prevention of trying to eliminate needing extra cash by working out the correct costs, the total budget and cost per person. It is essential if you are the team leader, as you cannot expect your team members to pay for your oversights/mistakes. Problems can arise when you delegate responsibilities to your host, who may not be quite so strict on finances as yourself. They may book accommodation, a worship team, transport, arrange for materials to be made or printed etc. and overspend.

Remember to keep all receipts, an account of all monies received, spent and given away. Write it down in a notebook. Issue receipts to members of the team each time they have made a payment towards the STM and keep the details in your notebook.

Chapter 15

Preparation Before you Depart

'Unless the Lord builds the house, they labour in vain who build it...'
(Psalm 127:1).

Long before you depart on your short-term mission (STM), do thorough research. If you joined a mission organization they will fill you in on all that you need to do (and know). Consider enrolling on an evening language course, especially if the destination you are going to speaks French, Spanish or Arabic. You can also buy a phrase book or language CDs, install them onto iTunes and put them onto your iPod or smartphone for quick reference, or get a translation App. Whilst English is spoken widely, learning another language or just essential phrases is a rewarding experience and any language study is a worthy investment. By putting more in now, you will get more out during your STM.

Learn some basic phrases in the local language:
- Hello.
- My name is.
- What is your name?
- Where is the toilet?
- How much?
- Where is the... hotel etc.
- Thank you.
- Goodbye etc.

Buy a pocket phrasebook. Consider enrolling on a First Aid course – a little bit of basic knowledge can be a lifesaver when you are a long way from help, or at least read a First Aid book to know the basics! If you are an independent STM-er (or the leader of any team) then you should know the basics of First Aid or someone on your team needs to know! If you are going to an extreme or isolated place (days from civilization or in harsh weather conditions/terrain) then consider enrolling on a basic survival course, or at least read a survival book and try to take it in! If it is pocketsize (e.g. Collins Gem *SAS Survival Guide*) take it with you.

Educate yourself about the country (and people) you will be going to. Buy a travel guide and read it. Find out the country's history, religion, culture, geography, climate (to include seasons – hot, cold, wet, humid), politics, cost of living, staple diet and types of accommodation if need be – each country has certain specific names, hotel, motel, B&B, inn, youth hostel, lodge, etc. If language is permissible, read their online papers to see what is happening in their country.

Physical and Spiritual Preparation

Make sure you are fit, your STM could be demanding and will probably not be a 9 till 5 day, sat in a swivel-chair inside an air-conditioned office, like many workplaces. Go out for a thirty-minute walk at least three times a week, do some exercise. I have known days on a STM where I have been on my feet all day, from 9am-7pm.

Pray for the mission: yourself, your leader, your team members (by name), your host, for Divine favour, protection, wisdom, discernment, confidence, boldness, health, for spiritual fruit, for favour, for Divine appointments, good interpreter, team cooperation, servant-heart and team dynamics etc. If you enjoy reading, then pick up some books about/by famous missionaries, be inspired.

Spend additional time with God, in prayer, listening to Him and in study of the Holy Bible. Your STM may be your first and only opportunity (hopefully not), and you must go as prepared as you can, give as much as you can and get as much out of it as you can; learn, make new friends and build your character.

Make sure all your electrical gadgets work. Are all your batteries charged? Do you know how to work your new digital camera, camcorder, smartphone or iPod? Have you bought your plug converter? Do you have the right clothing?

Types of Toilets

Toilets the world over are not the same. They may be Western type (the bowl and seat – though the seat is not always there), a bucket which you empty or the squat type (a hole in the ground) which are also known as long-drops. With the latter you squat down as there is no toilet seat to rest on. If there will be squat toilets in the country of your STM then practice squats to strengthen your thigh muscles and to aid balance – it will pay dividends by the time you arrive and have to use them. It may also tone your legs.

Mental Preparation

Your STM will be an amazing adventure, but if you go with the wrong attitude, you will miss the best that God has to offer. Go with the frame of mind that, "I am going to have a life changing trip – an opportunity of a lifetime!" There will be difficulties and perhaps some things that you will not like (even about yourself), or disapprove of, but nonetheless, if you are going in obedience to the Great Commission, to serve others you will get a lot out of it because you will put your all into it. Remind yourself, "I am going to go and embrace the experience and allow the experience to embrace and change me, and this may reveal any character flaws or weak areas I may have."

Expect the unexpected and don't be phased by it, as the unexpected can happen! Situations may not seem fun at the time, but are all part of the experience and turn into great stories for yourself and others!

The Leader's Reconnaissance Mission

The leader may consider flying to the host country from one year to eight months before the mission begins, though this may depend on the prospective number of team members, as there is a great difference in logistical planning between six or sixty team members! (See chapter 30, Working with the Locals). Discuss and submit your mission plans for evaluation – don't presume to know better than your host! The reconnaissance mission helps build up the relationship between the host leader, (local ministry or church fellowship) and the one who is planning the STM. They can see what resources are available, scout-out prospective accommodation, transport and cooking facilities (or places to eat) etc. and take some photos or video footage as these make recruiting for STMs easier.

If you are leading a STM team then make sure your team members know what is expected from them. Prepare any drama or mime sketches well. Those who are preaching or giving testimony, ensure they have ample notice to prepare. If you are involved in humanitarian work then be sure to pack what tools or equipment is needed. Distribute any tools or Christian materials throughout the team and remind them to pack it! Have all the team's passports with their visas arrived? Has every team member paid his or her money? Has the accommodation and plane's departure been confirmed? Is the church mini-bus and a driver still available to take you to the airport? Beware of double bookings!

Prepare and Worship as a Team

If you are going on a STM as a team then you should prepare as a team. The group, where possible should meet together once a week, for prayer, discussion, mission orientated Bible study etc., and things should be fully explained so that each individual knows what will be expected of them. If you are joining a mission organization, then there will probably be some training within your own country before you fly off to the destination of your mission. This helps you bond with other team members to prepare you for the STM.

As a STM team, it is beneficial to take some worship songbooks or some photocopies (copyright permitted) of your favourite worship songs, hymns or choruses which can be sung unaccompanied. A member of the team may wish to take their musical instrument along. Some instruments are delicate, expensive, or bulky. There may be a surcharge at the airport, as the instrument (e.g. guitar) may be processed through check-in as fragile and as a second bag; but try to take as hand luggage. It should be put in a strong protective case.

Research and Recommendations

In most major cities, there are people of different ethnic and cultural backgrounds. You may be able to begin your preparation for your STM by entering into some of these communities and meeting the type of people to whom you will be ministering and working alongside on your STM. If and where possible:

- Visit a church of a language group (or cultural group) similar to the country you will be visiting.
- Invite some of them to your home/church for dinner.
- Ask some of the church leaders for their advice, tips and help.
- Go to a restaurant of the country to whom you will be going and order some 'local' cuisine. For a church's STM team it is also a good way to get to know each other and bond.
- Rent a DVD, download a travel programme or search the internet for film clips of the travel destinations you will be going to. Visit Google Earth and explore.
- With the advent of digital radio (or via the internet) you may be able to listen to some 'local' radio from the comfort of your own room prior to your departure.

Prayer Support – It's Vital

Prayer support for your STM is essential and your local church should know *all about it* and you, unless you are going to a sensitive country. Key personnel can be informed but not the entire congregation. Be careful what you put in print. Long before you depart on your STM, you should ask your church to pray for you, and speak to whoever leads the weekly prayer and/or mission meetings. Send them a copy of your itinerary (if you have one) and keep them up to date. If possible, send regular emails back to your supporters and encourage and remind them that you value their prayers.

On your return home, remember to report back to your prayer supporters and tell them how things went – good or bad, but don't dwell on the negative. You may be given a five or ten minute slot to summarise your mission and to share answer to those prayers.

Chapter 16

Items to Buy and Consider

Jesus said to the disciples, "When I sent you without money bag, sack and sandals, did you lack anything?" So they said, "Nothing." Then He said to them, "But now, he who has a money bag, let him take it, and likewise a sack..." (Luke 22:35-36).

You're going on a short-term mission (STM) and you need to take some essential items with you. At a minimum, you will need a set of clothes and a bag; but at worse you will try to take several suitcases packed with all your favourite clothes; electrical goods and items that you 'just cannot' do without. When it comes to STMs, less is best – travel light. However, many STM teams take extra bags full of materials and supplies, which are used during the STM, or presents to give to the locals, your host and those who have assisted you.

Where you are going to and at what time of year dictates to you the type of clothing and items you will need. Where am I going to? What will the weather be like? If you know what the elements will be like (and you should know) then you can purchase items accordingly, however you probably have most items already. If it is hot then loose clothing is better, whereas if your location will be cold then multiple layers are more practical. Are you going in the rainy season? All these factors must be weighed and considered before you embark on your STM. Personally, I like to take clothes that wash easily (by hand) and dry quickly. I don't like wearing damp clothes and I need to know that my garments will dry well, even in winter, ideally within 8-12 hours. If you are staying in one place and there is an open-air clothesline, then it is not so much an issue.

Any mission organization of which you are signed up with will be able to inform you of your needs and will provide a recommended checklist of items to take.

The Best Deal

When it comes to items of clothing and a rucksack, I have always gone to a shop in person to try on the garment and examine the bag. Some items if purchased online can appear compact and light, but in reality, they can be heavy and cumbersome. Like most things, if you need something in a hurry then you will probably pay over the odds for it. Ask yourself, "Will my purchase accomplish the job for that which I need it?" You may also wish to consider with electrical items: Is it lightweight, compact, reliable and do I really need it on my STM? Sometimes it's nice to have an enforced break from a WiFi enabled device or smartphone; whilst at other times, they do come in rather handy, or quite essential. A mini laptop, WiFi enabled, Tablet, iPad or smartphone can be a good asset as many cafes, restaurants and accommodation have free WiFi.

There are many gadgets you can take on a STM, some will enhance your mission and help you remember the people you met and the places you went to. Whilst other items can be more of a distraction if abused, by isolating yourself from other members of the team and keeping you away from interacting with the locals. All items can be damaged, lost or stolen and so can their power sources. If you are with a mission organization or a church team staying in one location then the contents of your bag can be heavier than if you have to carry it on your back and travel frequently.

Digital Items to Consider

It is recommended to have a spare set of rechargeable batteries for your camera, cost and weight permitting. Is your iPod or digital voice recorder only chargeable via a USB port? Remember to take a plug adaptor with you, as you can generally only find them in the capitals of developing countries in more expensive hotel rooms.

In Asia, free WiFi in cafes and accommodation is quite common. Power cuts are a regular feature of developing countries. If on the internet, write short emails and send them as soon as you can. Charge your equipment when you can, for if you procrastinate, you may find that when you want to, you cannot!

If you like photography, take enough memory cards for your digital camera so that you will not be limited in what you can shoot. More is better and whilst memories will fade, pictures can last a lifetime.

Mobile/cell phones on the mission field can be a blessing but also a bane. They are great to have in an emergency but a bane to carry. It is another item that needs charging, which could get damaged or stolen and you may end up with a whopper of a phone bill. Some Pay as you Go phones do not work outside of their designated country. If you feel that a mobile is a necessity for your STM, then get a new SIM with cheap overseas deals or buy a local SIM card and email your number to your friends. On a STM of less than three weeks, I have generally taken a mobile/cell with me and the blessings have outweighed the disadvantages. Smartphones can also be great but be aware of huge data costs, turn off data roaming.

In many developing nations, there are telephone shops, which consist of numerous phone booths for calling, whilst budding entrepreneurs in marketplaces use their mobile/cell phones to make money. You could buy an international phone card or stick to WiFi.

Essential or Practical Items:

- Rucksack (backpack) or suitcase or holdall with wheels.
- A small day bag, ideal for taking on the plane as hand/carry-on luggage with your essential items.
- Money belt, an essential safety feature to protect your excess amounts of money, your passport and cash cards. NOT a bum-bag (fanny pack/belt bag). Women may prefer a neck wallet (a pouch that is hung round your neck), which is hidden under your top, a safe place for your passport or money. It is not as good as a money belt, but more practical if wearing a skirt or dress.
- Pocket calculator, which is reliable and sturdy.
- Breathable waterproof jacket (plastic raincoats make you sweat). If you are going to a cold and windy environment then you should consider it being windproof also.
- A sturdy pair of shoes or boots. If you are going into well below freezing temperatures, then specialist boots may be needed. Make sure you break any boots in before you depart.
- Scented foot insoles otherwise within a few weeks your footwear will stink! Think of your fellow STM-ers.
- Flip-flops (thongs) for the shower or for in your room. Most budget accommodation has dirty concrete floors. You do not want to get a verruca (or other foot viruses) by being barefoot in the shower or your room.
- A pair of sports sandals to give your feet breathing space if in warmer climates, can also be worn inside.
- Trousers (pants with zip-off legs are better) or skirt with zipped or velcro pockets (for security of your passport, wallet or purse) from any camping shop. Camouflage trousers are not advisable as you may be mistaken for military personnel. In some African countries, it is illegal for non-military to wear camouflage. In some Middle East countries, you DO NOT want to wear them!
- First Aid kit. For an individual it is often better to make your own First Aid kit rather than buy an off-the-shelf one; visit your local chemist. Team leaders should buy a big one and add to it. An individual should take plenty of plasters (Band Aids), two bandages, antiseptic cream, safety pins and some medicines at a minimum. Safety pins have multiple purposes like holding your bag together, keeping your trousers (pants) up if you are not good at using a needle and thread, or have just lost your button or broken your flies/zipper. If you are going to be doing a lot of walking, consider taking fungicidal cream.

- Mini Sewing Kit (matchbox size) which includes a few needles and various colours of thread.
- Small lightweight torch (flashlight). LED lights are more powerful. Headlight type torches are more practical than handheld ones because of power cuts (early mornings and at night), just when you are trying to pack your bag! Windup LED key ring torches are available.
- Cheap digital watch with alarm, day and date, built in light and ideally waterproof. It is easy to lose track of time and with early buses or trains to catch before sunrise, I have found a digital watch indispensible on STMs. If it does not have a light, you will be constantly waking up on the day of your departure trying to find your torch.
- Latest guidebook, backpackers type, I have always found useful for the cost of transport, accommodation, bus routes, food, scams to beware of, border crossings and visa costs etc.
- Pocket-sized phrase book is useful when you are ministering in one location. You may have a translation App on your smartphone.
- Journal – A5 spiral pad and a pen, or an iPad, Tablet or mini laptop/notebook + plug adaptor and power cable.
- Travel towel (micro-fibre type), they are very light.
- Sun cream, sunhat, moisturiser & lip balm with UV protection.
- Compact umbrella to protect from rain and intense sun.
- Locks (key or combination) for your rucksack and 2 small ones for your side pockets. One medium sized lock for a hotel cupboard or for your room's door (especially in cheap accommodation).
- Small pocketknife with scissors and tweezers at a minimum. This CANNOT be taken aboard a plane as hand luggage, or any sharp objects, liquids, creams and aerosols over 100ml. Do you need mosquito repellent? It should contain DEET.
- Small handheld mirror, a flip one is added protection
- Travel sickness pills/tablets, they can also take the edge off a long journey to help you sleep.
- Toiletries: deodorants, toothbrush, creams, feminine hygiene products, razor (or shaver), headache tablets, nail clippers, shampoo, toothpaste etc. Most of these items can also be bought on arrival. Share your toothpaste with a friend.
- Prescription for medicines and a spare pair of glasses. It would be unfortunate to go on a STM and have to wait till you return home to check your photos to see what your STM looked like in focus!

One or other of the following:
- Silk bag liner or a lightweight 750-gram sleeping bag for basic or cold accommodation.
- Space/foil blanket, a pocket sized foil blanket that can be used in emergencies – or when cold!
- General sleeping bag, will you be camping? What rating do you need? The higher the rating the warmer and heavier the sleeping bag.

Do you need:
- A tent. A three-man tent is ideal for two people and their bags. The lighter and more compact a tent is the more expensive they are. If you both have individual tents (not recommended) then you will have to rent two pitches, a false economy.
- Do you need to take a cooking stove, gas cylinders, plastic mug, plate and cutlery etc.?
- Backpack cage for added security, especially if staying in a youth hostel with strangers, or on a night train. Downside is the weight, up to ½ kg.

Items Which you May Like to Take

Many of the items on this list are of personal preference:
- Compact video camera (+ tapes or SD cards) or smartphone.
- A digital camera and plenty of memory cards.
- Rechargeable batteries for your camera (if needed), plus a spare set and a fast battery charger.
- Plug adaptor for the country you are going to and a shaver adaptor (two-pinned plug). Very important items.
- Personal Entertainment: iPod or MP3/4 player or ereader.
- Mini laptop WiFi enabled, (10 inch screen and cable can weight just 1.6 kg). An iPad, Tablet or smartphone is a lot lighter and may also be used in photography and/or video.
- Travel kettle with a plug (and not a 6-volt car adaptor). Some are supplied with two cups that fit inside the kettle. Great for tea, coffee, soups and for instant noodles.
- A rechargeable shaver (unless you prefer wet shaves).
- A hair dryer (you may be able to use a friend's, so pair up with a friend and reduce the weight of your bag).

Other items to consider:
- Plastic bowl for noodles, cereals or instant soup.
- Plastic spoon and fork (as a single item) or chopsticks.
- Plastic cup (if not included with your travel kettle).
- Six pegs (clothespins), for your washing and for holding curtains closed!

- Thin string (5-8 metres) – which can be used as a washing line (clothesline) or for holding things together.
- Spare pair of shoelaces for walking boots – after several hard weeks or months they can break at any time.
- Four A4 plastic wallets to keep documents safe and dry.
- Plastic or wooden doorstop, a great security device for when you are inside your cheap hotel room. (You can also half fill a plastic bottle with water and put it on your door handle. If someone tries to get in, it will fall on the floor and wake you up!).
- A gift(s) for your host and small gifts for when you are invited to someone's home for a meal.
- Change, so that you can phone home on your return.
- A photo of your loved one(s) who is at home.

Prescription Medicines

It is important that you keep all medicines in their original packaging with the accompanying pamphlet. These pamphlets also state the medical composition of the tablets or capsules and so make it easier for the pharmacist abroad to issue you with what you need; not all medicines are generic and Western brand names may not exist in some countries. Some medicines may require a letter from your doctor if you intend on passing through customs unhindered (ask your doctor). Some (prescription) medicines in the West (e.g. codeine, for pain relief) are illegal in some countries.

Designer Labels, Jewellery and Robbers

Whilst most people like to look good, on a STM it is advisable that you leave your bling at home. Chunky chains, gold watches, excessive jewellery, fancy handbags and designer labels are not practical and can alienate you from those you are trying to reach. They also make you standout as a target to rob.

If in the unfortunate event that you do get confronted by robbers with knives or guns, do not resist, let them take your wallet/purse, camera or mobile/cell phone if they ask for it. They are probably just as scared as you, but if you resist or refuse, they may react by instinct and you could be injured. It is not worth it, let your material possessions go and save yourself. Discretion is the better part of valour – it is often wise to refrain from seemingly brave speech or action in distressing circumstances. Report any theft to the local police and get a report filled out for an insurance claim. On the last day of a STM in Tunisia, my friend had his jacket stolen from on top of his bag which he was carrying! The policeman explained that if they caught the thief we would have to attend the court hearing. I told my friend to forgot it, we fly home in twelve hours.

Chapter 17

Go Pack your Bag

Jesus said to the disciples... "But now, he who has a money bag, let him take it, and likewise a sack..." (Luke 22:36).

When it comes to clothes, within reason it is up to you what you want to take on your short-term mission (STM), though if you are going with an organization they will advise you of what you need and give a general idea of how many of each items. However, before you decide what to take; you will need a good backpack (rucksack), bag, suitcase or holdall to put it all in.

Items to Consider with your Bag
The bag that you will take on your STM is a vital component and there are many factors involved, but with some simple logical questions and answers, it will help you get the right rucksack, bag, suitcase, or holdall for you:
- Will it go as hand/carry-on luggage?
- Can I carry the bag when full?
- Will I be transporting heavy materials?
- Is it more practical to carry the bag on my back?
- Will I be constantly travelling on public transport?
- Will I be staying in one place or multiple locations?

Your Bag
Rucksacks/backpacks are my preferred choice of bag for STMs, though when I had to take large quantities of Christian materials (Bibles, videos, pamphlets etc.) I used a suitcase with wheels. I have never come across the perfect rucksack.

Rucksack capacities are measured in litres/liters (L):
- 20-30L is a standard day-bag backpack.
- 35+8L is what I first took to South-East Asia (and it was very small).
- 50+10L is what I used in Africa for 6 ½ months and on my second STM to Asia. It is my personal preferred size.

Anything above 60+10L may be too big to carry and a hindrance on public transport and anything above 80L is just excessive. However if you are in a single location, and therefore not travelling regularly on public transport with your bag, it does not matter as much. There is nothing wrong with having a bigger bag except you may be tempted to fill it to its brim. Whatever rucksack, bag, suitcase or holdall you buy, make sure you can carry it when packed (or someone can), and that it does not exceed the airline's baggage allowance! If you cannot carry it up a flight of stairs or lift it above your head to stow on a bus then you may have packed too many items.

If you are going on a mission to one fixed location and leaving items behind, then the weight and size of your bag (except the airline's baggage allowance) is also not an issue. Airline baggage allowance varies between airlines (and between countries) though 15-23 kilograms (kg) for check-in items and 5-7 kg for hand/carry-on luggage is a general rule. If you exceed your baggage weight allowance, you will have to pay an excess baggage charge, which varies considerably and can be quite large. Airlines can be flexible with charities and groups *if* you speak to them in advance.

If you have a weak or bad back then a suitcase on wheels may be better, but it's no fun pulling them through the mud in the rainy season! If you think a suitcase is best for you then ask yourself, "Do I need wheels?" and, "Does it need to be a hard case?" Hard cases are heavier than soft cases and offer more protection for fragile items, but they have no give in them when trying to store in an overhead bus rack or under the seat and weigh more, though they can be used as a seat! Does your bag need to be lockable? Do I need compartments? Expensive luggage does not mean better or sturdier.

Practical Clothing – Not Problematic

Remember that you are going on a mission and not a fashion parade. What may be trendy or acceptable at home may not be practical or appropriate where you are going. It is possible to alienate the people you are trying to reach simply because your normal day-to-day clothes are too good or that you have a change of clothes for each day and others do not. Remember to bring something smart to wear to the local church and jeans are not a good option in most parts of the world. In some deprived areas, STM teams have found that their work clothes have been better than many of the locals' Sunday best.

Look presentable when passing through border crossings, otherwise you could be turned away as undesirable! There is no need to wear a suit, but just be clean and smart.

The clothes you pack should reflect the type of climate you are going to. Take modest swimwear, as you never know when you may have the opportunity for a dip, use of a hot tub or a warm spring. Remember your wide rimmed sun hat if your ears are prone to burn, a long sleeved shirt to protect your arms from sunburn and by upturning your shirt's collar your neck is preserved from going red. Do you need to bring a pair of sunglasses/shades? In Africa and Asia they are frequently sold on the streets for around £1.90 ($3).

Beware of having clothes that reveal too much. Even in some countries, it is frowned upon, or even forbidden for women to reveal their shoulders or upper arms in public. Muslim countries are not enthusiastic with men wearing shorts above the knee. There are always exceptions to the rule, especially in tourist towns, but a betrayal towards the feelings of others to whom we are trying to reach may cause them to reject not only us, but also our message. Since the Arab Spring (2011) across parts of North Africa and some Middle East countries, the rule of law has broken down (or is in transition) and women are more vulnerable than ever before. Don't wear tight clothes.

Wrong colours such as light green and light brown can show up sweat marks (or become see-through) and thus reveal, in sweaty climates patches of dark material, which can be quite embarrassing. Zipped or pockets with velcro are essential as a prevention from being pick-pocketed. Trousers/pants with zip off legs are handy, but set security metal detectors off! Patriotic clothing is best avoided (national flags etc.) as is military clothing and camouflage.

Lightweight Clothes List

The clothes within this list are a general guide and the quantity includes what you may wear on the plane, one set of clothes, your jacket and a sturdy pair of boots. I wear XXL clothes, which takes up more room than a size 14 and I travel light. Extra items that you deem most practical should be packed, but leave some space in your bag for items you purchase whilst on your STM. As a good rule of STMs – pack less, wash your clothes frequently and take items that are relevant to your destination's weather conditions. The following is a lightweight list and what you should take as a minimum:

- T-shirt x 2
- Working shirt or blouse x 2
- Trousers (pants) or skirts x 2
- Smart shirt/blouse x 1
- Zipped fleece jumper (sweater) x 1
- Waterproof jacket x 1
- Underwear x 4+
- Socks x 4+
- Hat, scarf and gloves x 1 (if applicable)
- A pair of sturdy boots
- A pair of sports sandals (if applicable)

- A pair of flip-flops (thongs)
- Shorts x 1
- Swimwear x 1
- Nightwear x 1 (or just a t-shirt and shorts)

Packing your Items and Team Materials

Before you pack, lay all your items out on your bed or on the floor, to see if you have everything (use a list and tick it off). Ideally, take two of each items: t-shirt, trousers (pants) or skirts, (more for underwear), but only one jacket and one pair of flip-flops (thongs), and sandals. Remember, you will be wearing one set of clothes with you and can buy additional items whilst on your STM. Don't forget to pack your Bible and any sermons you have prepared.

Don't pack revealing items, tight clothing or those that you *really* cannot live without (they may get damaged) and any other forms of impractical clothing. Do you need to buy some small presents/gifts for your host or if you are invited to someone's house for a meal? In many cultures, if they invite you into their home, a gift is expected and those from home, mean more than locally bought items. Small trinkets/souvenirs are appreciated.

If you are part of a mission organization, you may be asked to pack some team materials in your bag. Christian tracts, pamphlets, videos, DVDs, CDs, or Bibles and medicines etc., plus other equipment including work tools and quality clothes to give away. This evens out the weight and minimises loss if a bag is lost in transit. If items were in a single bag you may be stopped at customs as a mobile library, pharmacist (bring correct paperwork – if needed) or a sales agent who is trying to avoid paying duty and taxes on the goods which they believe you are going to sell.

Some mission teams like to have team t-shirts – it may be cute; helps identify a group of relative strangers as one, but at times it is not practical and can be unwise. If you are passing through customs with all your materials, if one of you is stopped, and the official is not happy with your contents of Bibles or tools, then don't be surprised if you *all* get stopped and everybody's luggage is searched. This can be time consuming and hard to re-pack.

Many items have been listed in this chapter and the previous one, but with careful packing, the vast majority of the items mentioned (excluding a tent, standard sleeping bag and video camera) can fit into a reasonably sized rucksack alongside a *small* carry-on bag. (I use a micro-sleeping bag that weighs just 750 grams). You have to pack your bag intelligently and utilise your space. It is not uncommon to pack and unpack your rucksack or suitcase up to three times, as you juggle items and remove others. If you need two large bags to pack all your items then you have far too much!

Remember you may need space to pack team materials! Wear heavy and bulky items on the plane. If you take a book about STMs into a sensitive country, you may want to put a dustcover/jacket from another book on it. ☺

Documents and Hand/Carry-On Luggage

All essential or valuable items should be packed in a day bag and taken on the plane as hand/carry-on luggage. Your rucksack or suitcase will be checked in at the airport. It should be at baggage reclaim when you are, but not always! You can always wear your heavier or bulky items (jeans, big boots, and jumper/sweater, and jacket) with you onto the plane instead of packing them.

Do not forget to pack photocopies (xerox) of important documents (valid passport, medical insurance, plane ticket (and visa) in clear A4 plastic wallets), your guidebook (if needed), Bible, medicines and some passport size photos – they may be required for a visa on arrival (future visas) or given to your new friends! All of your valuables, journal, pen, laptop, mobile/cell phone and essentials should go as hand luggage. Some people recommend a change of clothes and a toothbrush in case your bag is waylaid or lost.

Social Networks

Social networks can be a good means of communication, but also a dangerous and foolish means of letting the world know what you are doing, where and when. To be "quiet" is a huge discipline, but can prevent trouble, for you and for future STM teams. Remember, not all your social media "friends" are friends, or Christian, some are old acquaintances, people who you used to go to school with, others you may not be familiar with! Some contacts, you have never had face-to-face contact with! Be cautious of uploading data-tagged images from smartphones and digital cameras with the GPS function turned on. It is probably best to avoid a running day-to-day commentary on your blog or social media account and much of what happens should not be written about (places, names, especially leaders and other contacts). What does your leader say and what is the policy of the mission organization?

There may be people and governments who object to STMs (in the sensitive country) where you are going to who search social media sites. Some also use search engines in general to try and catch and then expel these people from their country. Should you be writing about your STM (before, during or after) on social media when your account setting is not private and some friends are non-Christian?

Chapter 18

Preparing for Departure

'Those who are wise shall shine like the brightness of the firmament and those who turn many to righteousness like the stars forever and ever' (Daniel 12:3).

Three days before departure, check online or phone up the airline to confirm the time of the flight as sometimes they change. Make sure you know how you are getting to the airport! Do you need a map, or does the Sat Nav work? Do you need to send a SMS/text to the team to remind them when and where to meet? Pack your bags and weigh them. Do not exceed the airline bag and weight policy.

On the day before departure, double-check your hand/carry-on luggage and that you have your passport, money and plane tickets with you. Fully charge all electronic items. If you are driving to the airport in the church's minibus, are all the tyres inflated? Has the oil, coolant and screen-wash been checked? If you are part of a mission organization, you may have already done some orientation and/or training at a base before you depart.

You may be able to check-in online 24hrs before departure and pick your seat on the plane. Do this as a team and try and sit together if possible, or at least with one other person. If you are flying as a team, you may be meeting up at the airport, or at church and taking the minibus to the airport. Don't be late.

On the day of departure, leave in plenty of time, as it is better to wait around for three hours at the airport (you have to be there at least two hours in advance) than to miss the flight because the minibus broke down or the train was delayed. Keep your plane ticket and passport on you!

Airport Arrival and Etiquette

You may have travelled abroad before, but there is always a first time at the airport. Airports are high security risk areas; do not joke about guns, bombs, terrorism or diseases. It may get you arrested, detained or banned from the flight. Do not leave luggage unattended.

- Arrive in plenty of time and look presentable.
- If part of a team, do not be loud and boisterous. Do not block gangways and do not go wandering off.
- Check-in (if you have not done it online) at the airport desk with the airline you are flying with and receive your Boarding Card.

Your visa may be checked to see if you are entitled to enter the country you are going to. Or you may just be 'in transit' as you have to get a second flight. Try to check-in as a group and get seats near each other. Have passports and tickets to hand. If you have special dietary requirements (for your free meal on the plane) mention it to the staff. Check your luggage in at the same desk, your bag will be weighed. Dangerous items such as penknife, scissors, nail file, nail clippers, deodorants cans and creams and fluids in excess of 100ml should be in your check-in luggage, NOT your hand/carry-on luggage. Airlines have many other restrictions and prohibited items (which change from time to time) but liquids, creams and deodorants of *more than* 100ml each are forbidden, though you can purchase the latter items once you have passed through the Secure Area of the airport. Do not have any loose straps on your luggage as they can get caught and rip your bag. At check-in you may be asked if you packed your own bag, "Yes," and has it been left unattended, "No." You will receive a receipt for your bag; the airline worker at check-in may stick it to the back of your Boarding Card. This proves that you have luggage. You may need to show it in the country of arrival when you depart from the airport. A reminder: Do NOT joke about bombs, terrorism, guns, Ebola or other contagious diseases.

- If the group is taking a musical instrument, try to take on the plane as hand/carry-on luggage, as it may get damaged. If not, process it through check-in as a fragile item. Often you have to take it to a separate desk to be processed.
- If the plane's departure is delayed, phone your host as he or she may be waiting around for some time.

Moving Through the Airport
- Once you have done check-in and your luggage has been taken, say your goodbyes and go through to the Secure Area of Departures. Have your passport and Boarding Card ready for inspection. There will be a bin where all barred items (scissors, creams, fluids etc.) have to be left behind and never seen again. Creams, fluids and deodorants of less than 100ml have to be placed together in a resealable transparent bag no bigger than 20cm x 20cm, separate from your carry-on luggage.
- Now you have to go through security. Empty your pockets and put your hand luggage in the boxes on the conveyer belt where it will go through an x-ray machine. Camera film and tapes should be OK. You may have to turn your electronic items on (ereader, mobile/cell phone, laptop etc.). If you cannot prove that they work, you may not be permitted to take them aboard. If you

are wearing boots, a jacket, belt, coat or a hat you will probably have to remove them before passing through the other side of the secure area. Staff or signs will notify you of this. Remove all coins, keys and electrical items before you walk through the metal detector/scanner (which looks like a metal doorframe). If the machine beeps, the security guard (Transportation Security Administration in the U.S., an agency of Homeland Security) will scan you with a handheld scanner and/or frisk you. You may have to empty your pockets. In April 2016, it was revealed that bras from a UK high-street retailer were setting off airport scanners due to the amount of metal in the underwire! A money belt full of wads of notes can also be an issue, just let them know what it is, and you will probably have to remove it. Do not let it out of your sight! (With the rise of terrorists and suicide belts, money belts are becoming more problematic). If the guard cannot find the offending item, you may have to go for a full body scan in a separate room. You keep your clothes on. Take your hand/carry-on luggage with you, which has gone through the x-ray machine. Travel/walking trousers with metal zipped pockets (I have seven zips on mine) are problematic at airports, as they always set the machine off and the guards may get nervous (as they did when I was in Pakistan). They cannot find anything and think that something is being concealed.

- You may also encounter sniffer dogs which are trained to pick up the scent of drugs, explosives or other contraband.
- After you have passed through security there may be time to shop, to buy a drink or have a snack.
- Get to the Departures Gate in plenty of time to board your plane. Use the bathroom/restroom *before* you board your plane. You will need to show your Boarding Card and passport before you can board the plane. Sometimes passengers with certain seat numbers are called first. There will be toilets on the plane, but aircrew do not like you using them when they are on the ground and you may be 'grounded' for some time.
- Find your seat on the plane, store your carry-on bag in the overhead compartment. See where the safety exits are.
- On the plane, you may be able to watch a movie on the in-flight entertainment system. Hopefully there will be complimentary drinks and a meal or two, depending on the length of your flight. Have a good sleep if you can.
- With most countries, you will have to fill out an Arrivals Card. These are issued on the plane or at Immigration, have a pen handy. Fill in your name, passport number and answer the questions. You may have to declare how much money you are bringing in to the country. I have always been cautious about

this (especially at land borders) so that I am not robbed. Under the 'Nature of Visit' (Business or Pleasure), you are a tourist (unless you have a business visa for your STM), as you are not going to make money or trade. You may have to return your half of the Arrivals Card on your departure, so keep it safe, alongside your Boarding Card.

Arriving at a New Country

- Arriving at your destination by plane you will have to collect your bag and then go through Immigration. Make sure you collect your bag, and not one that looks like yours! You may be able to get a trolley to put your bag on which saves carrying it. Or pile the team's bags onto several trolleys. On occasions, bags do get lost or arrive on a later plane. Contact the airline from inside the airport and they will generally forward your bag on to you.
- Go through customs and you should not have anything to declare, walk through the green channel (Nothing to Declare). If there are two gates, the other will be Items to Declare and will be red. Your bag may be checked at customs but unlikely. Often they do random searches. If you are taking in Christian materials (e.g. Bibles and tracts) into a sensitive country you should not go through customs as a group, but as individuals or pairs. You could pass through with a family, walk close behind them!
- You now have to pass through Immigration where you show your passport and visa (if needed). Or just before Immigration you can buy your visa if you do not need to apply for one and/or fill in an Immigration Card. If you are in a sensitive country, you might want to go through interspersed with other arrivals.
- At Immigration, hand your passport over. The officer on duty, will look at your passport (maybe scan it) and look at you. He or she may ask you some questions, or just stamp your passport and let you into the country. Adhere to all rules and regulations. If there is a health scare like Ebola, you may be screened (questions will be asked and your temperature taken).
- Arriving at your destination can be exciting, but your journey through different time zones can upset your senses and dampen your emotional well-being. You may not have rested on your ten-hour night flight or you could be unwell because of turbulence.
- Do you need to exchange some money at the airport, or is there an ATM/cash point where you can withdraw the local currency?
- Make sure the team is together, keep an eye on everyone, beware of touts/hustlers. Have all the bags been collected and is everyone present? Do not let strangers take your bags to their transport. They may want payment for carrying your bags to an expensive taxi! Take some transport to your accommodation.

Chapter 19

The Arrival

'May the Lord watch between you and me when we are absent one from another' (Genesis 31:49).

After you clear customs and enter a new world, you should at least try to pretend that you know what you are doing; though if you are with a mission organization, many pressures (of finding transport and accommodation) are alleviated. Try to use the bathrooms/ restrooms before you leave the airport. Foreigners are most vulnerable when they first arrive at a new destination. Whether you have come by plane, ship or across a land border, passing from where you have come from to a new country or district does make you stand out. Be aware of your surroundings.

Stepping through the airport doors with a fresh visa and stamp on your passport (or when arriving at a bus, train or ferry terminal) touts and hustlers can quickly latch on to the foreigner, offering their assistance; sometimes they are helpful, at other times they are not! Be polite; do not feel obligated to enter into a conversation. If you are with an organization, stick close to your leader and keep an eye out for your fellow team members. Do a head count, are all present? Make sure *all* your luggage goes into the taxi or bus.

Border crossings are the most wary places to be, but especially as you emerge from no-man's-land and into a new country where more often than not, you will be swarmed upon like bees to an open pot of jam/jelly. Do not believe everything that you are told by people who want to take your money. "The hotel is closed," "the road is un-driveable," "it is flooded," "there are no buses, till next week, I'll take you in my taxi," "the taximeter is broken" etc. are comments that you may hear by people who want you to use their services.

However much you prepare for your arrival at your new destination you can be easily caught unaware, as expectation and reality can be far apart. On the journey to your "new home" there are new sights, sounds, smells and even stirred emotions, which may be hard to take in, thoughts of those you left behind and possible jetlag. Like everything, it does take time to settle in and to recover from a journey, especially if you have crossed time zones, but after a few days your body will readjust and everything will get back to normal.

You may not be initially impressed with your new dwelling place, which may be yours for a considerable amount of time, but count your blessings, you have a roof over your head, you will get fed at regular intervals and you have a job to do. Check your bed sheets or sleeping bag before you get in – just in case of creepy crawlies! Shakeout your clothes in the morning and check your shoes for unwanted guests! Keep on top of your hygiene.

I would encourage you to read in addition to your normal Bible reading, a chapter of Proverbs and Ephesians everyday whilst you are on your short-term mission (STM), and don't neglect your quiet times with God (Bible reading and prayer).

If you are with a mission organization, your arrival will be much easier than if you 'go it alone' with a friend (independent STM) as everything is prearranged, from transport to accommodation. For everyone else, there may be problems with the language, money exchange (for some countries you can only buy currency within the country), airport taxi drivers (always a few who try to take advantage), the unfamiliar surroundings and the primary object of finding a place to stay, a hotel, motel, youth hostel, guesthouse, lodge or B&B. You will also meet touts, some are very helpful, others are a pain.

You may have just arrived at your destination or after a week think that you have made a major mistake and want to quit. Don't run away and go home or begin to murmur and complain! People may have made sacrifices to help finance your STM, and people need to hear the Good News. Never run away from the organization that you are part of or quit your STM because the going has got tough; you will regret it and will have missed a valuable life lesson, which you will have to learn at another time. Often God allows things to be difficult to help refine our character. If you are feeling low, look at a photo of those who are most special to you (keep it in your wallet/purse or on your smartphone) and remember the good times. You will get to see them again. Talk it over with your leader and leaders prepare!

Homesickness can set in after several months, but can be after just a few weeks. You are more prone to being homesick if you have never spent time away from your family.

> 'And say to Archippus, "Take heed to the ministry which you have received in the Lord, that you may fulfil it" ' (Colossians 4:17).

Women on Missions

Women on the mission field, but especially young women may encounter problems on their STM, which their male counterpart will not. Call me old fashioned, but Christian men (including teenagers) should look out for their sisters in the Lord and be there to protect them from men who are not part of the STM team or church fellowship. Especially on the streets or on public transport. Some women will be looked down upon because of their age and gender, whilst some locals will greatly respect, value and appreciate their service to those to whom they hold no blood or ethnic tie.

Medical Problems and Healthcare

Medical problems can be an issue in developing countries. The nearest hospital may be a long way away and the facilities may not be what you are used to, however some hospitals have incredible facilities and highly skilled staff.

If you need medical assistance, try and contact your medical insurance company/travel insurance first. They may tell you to go to an approved hospital or a surgery. If this is not possible, be cautious of blood transfusions (has it been screened?). If you need an injection, is the syringe new? Have you watched the doctor or nurse take it out of its sealed package? If you are unconscious, you cannot do any of the above, but hopefully a senior member of the STM team will be able to speak to those in charge or sign the various consent forms on your behalf. Keep all receipts to be reimbursed by your insurer. God-willing, you will never encounter these situations, but it is good to know about them.

In extremely cold weather, exposed skin but especially your nose and fingers (as well as your toes) can freeze, giving rise to frostbite. If the temperature is in double digits below zero, metal watchstraps in direct contact with the skin can freeze to the skin. Cold weather with piercing winds or freezing/driving rain can also cut skin. Wear lots of thin layers of clothing to help keep you warm.

If you are exposed to the sun (or just UV rays) then sunburn and/or heatstroke can cause major problems. Cover up exposed skin and drink plenty of water. Find some shade.

Squat and Bush Toilets

The stench in some outside squat toilets can be nauseating, with flies buzzing and maggots wriggling! The floors can be slippery and often there is no light and never any toilet paper; with the idea being that you wipe yourself with the left hand (or you provide your own paper!), pour water down the hole and then wash your hands with water as there will be no soap! There is often a tap/faucet or a bowl of water where you pour some water down the hole and let water displacement take care of the rest.

Some toilets are in the bush and it is customary to dig a little hole and cover up after yourself. If the bus/coach stops after a few hours on a dirt road, with no building in sight, then the men go to one side of the road and the women to the other side, and aftertime you will feel quite at home in the wilds of Africa or parts of Asia.

Journal, Daily Budgeting and Receipts

I would encourage anybody who goes on a STM to keep a journal, however brief, even if just a short paragraph per day. The weakest ink is better than the strongest memory. However, be aware that writing a detailed journal in a sensitive country could be incriminating evidence against you, your team and those you have ministered with and to! In my A5 spiral bound journals (a new one for each STM) I keep a daily record of all the places that I have been, what I have eaten or seen, observations, how I feel and the day's expenses. A journal is interesting to read when you go through what you did each day, one year on from the STM and after several years, you can pick it up as a travel adventure and the memories will come flooding back.

Daily, I tally up the expenses (accommodation, food and drink, travel for the team) and then add them together to form the week's expenses and then add up the monthly budget. I can keep a tight tab of the mission budget and if we have overspent one week, we have to make cuts the following week. The monthly tallies are recorded at the back of my journal alongside all the money exchanged and withdrawals at cash points/ATMs with a separate list for money which is given to Christian workers (interpreter, evangelist, pastor etc.) or love gifts to Christian ministries/organizations (schools orphanages, money for Bibles or other Christian materials etc.). I have found that this method is the most practical when it comes to balancing the books. Due to exchange rates there are always minor differences.

A mission leader should keep a tight tab on the team's budget and some will carry a notebook to write down all the costs of the team, which is wise. Where possible keep receipts (especially in regards to accommodation, transport, food, materials as well as gifts) as you may have to submit them to the church treasurer. Many cafes, restaurants, shops and stalls do not issue receipts (sometimes you just have to ask), and when they do, remember to calculate how much it costs in your home currency and write it on the receipt.

Social Networks and Big Brother

Do not share your problems or vent your frustrations on social networks. Many a person has had to try and back peddle their comments (and apologies) after writing a comment or changing their status. It is also unwise to let the world know what you are doing, where and when. Your online 'friends' whom you may have never met, may not be your friends! Is your status private? What is the mission organization's policy on social media? Are you a keen blogger? Should you be telling the world of your exploits or be keeping things vague? What does your leader say?

Many modern digital cameras are WiFi enabled (as are smartphone) and so photos can be uploaded directly to social media sites, but beware of giving away what you are doing in sensitive countries and avoid uploading. If in doubt, check with your leader. Many digital cameras (and smartphones) also have GPS (Global Positioning System), where images are data-tagged with the latitude and longitude of your location. You may wish to turn the GPS off, before you take a photo if you intend to upload the photo. What is the mission organization's policy?

As a word of warning, smartphones can be very handy, but expensive to run when abroad, turn off data roaming and automatic updates. Phone signals can be tracked by triangulation whilst some smartphones are the ultimate GPS tracking beacons! Big brother may be watching you!

Internet Banking and Internet Cafes

You should be very cautious of using online banking from an internet cafe (especially in developing countries) or cheap hotel and try to avoid making purchases online. A programme could be collecting all your details. If you have your own laptop, Tablets or smartphone then it is safer (but not immune to cyber attacks and theft). Do not get paranoid, just be aware of these things.

If you are not using your own device then remember to 'Log Out' after all applications where you have had to enter a password to access information, even your email account. Do not click, 'Remember Me.' Or, 'Keep Me Signed In,' unclick the button if it automatically defaults to that setting. After you have logged out, you should delete the computer's history, information that remains within the computer's memory such as websites visited and passwords. With your internet browser open, delete your browsing history, temporary internet files, form data and passwords etc.

I have been on many computers in internet cafes and have been quite surprised at what I have found in Documents, the personal files that people have written and left on the computer's hard drive; business proposals, completed job interview forms etc. If you write a file on a public computer, save onto a USB stick and delete the file on the computer.

'Go in peace. May the presence of the Lord be with you on your way' (Judges 18:6).

Chapter 20

Duty and Character

'Brethren, pray for us, that the Word of the Lord may have free course and be glorified, just as it is with you' (2 Thessalonians 3:1).

You have arrived at your final destination to begin your short-term mission (STM). You have been allocated a room; you've met your roommate(s); your bag is unpacked (or on the floor by your bed) and now is not the time to go wandering off! You are probably part of a STM team, having joined a mission organization and there will need to be a team/group meeting. Listen to the leader(s) and follow their instruction. Some ground rules will need to be stated and words of wisdom imparted; introductions to members of the team (who did not travel with you), and staff members who live on site, followed by a tour of the mission facilities (if it's not just a hotel or hostel).

If you have not joined a mission organization the first thing to do is to find a place to stay; if you have not already pre-booked a room in a cheap hotel or youth hostel. You will probably want to shower up, perhaps have a brief rest and then go outside and familiarise yourself with your local surroundings. Grab hold of a business card of your accommodation – just in case you get lost!

Depending on how long your STM is (2 weeks to 1 year), the state you are in (jetlagged or just plain exhausted) and your condition (or that of the team) will often dictate whether you start your STM on the day of your arrival or whether it begins on the following day.

There are lots of things to do when you are in the country of destination, but a few things to do when you have settled in are:

- Familiarise yourself with your local surroundings. Look for landmarks. Do not run off, but get (or give) permission.
- Go out and meet the locals – a must do on any STM!
- Visit different churches (if permissible).
- Try the local cuisine and drinks (non-alcoholic).
- Having your hair cut in another country is always interesting and is good for social interaction. But be aware that your words may get lost in translation and your hair style could drastically alter with a single snip of the scissors!
- Haggle with street sellers (but don't financially beat them up). It is enjoyable, educational and you will hopefully buy something that you like, need or will use as a gift for another.
- Listen to the local radio, if there is one available.

- Watch the local TV programmes if possible, but especially the news and local affairs programmes.

'Thus says the Lord God, "Although I have cast them far off among the Gentiles, and although I have scattered them among the countries, yet I shall be a little sanctuary for them in the countries where they have gone" ' (Ezekiel 11:16).

Your Room, Your Home, Your Chores
You have been allocated a room (or a bed in a room); try to keep it tidy! Remember your mum/mom will not be there to clean up behind you. Even if you are in a hotel or guesthouse; use the bin/trash can and do not *expect* the cleaners to pick up your rubbish because you could not be bothered to put it in the bin/trash can. Be Christ-like. Remember, you don't know who will pay you a visit or just pop in. The same applies for when you rent an apartment or house for the STM team.

Report any breakages to your leader (or host) and don't let it be a surprise for your host or mission organization when you have departed! The quality of furniture varies from place to place and the bench that can hold four petite Asian women may not hold two burly Westerners. Don't put damp clothes on varnished furniture – the lacquer may lift. Don't tramp mud through the home.

It is very unwise to leave valuables lying around – do not tempt the cleaner or others. I have stayed in 100s of different places and only once was something stolen from my room – lip balm. Someone had a greater need than myself and I was able to laugh it off. In hostels (amongst fellow foreigners), things go missing; and are more likely to. Never leave bulk materials, e.g. tracts, videos, DVDs, Bibles, CDs etc. lying around in your hotel room, especially if you are in a sensitive country where evangelising is illegal or questionable. The hotel cleaner may inform the manager who could inform the authorities and you will get to hear about it! Some countries state that there is freedom of religion, but often the reality is very different and open to interpretation under local bylaws or the police person in charge!

As part of a mission team; you are going to have to do duties and chores, perhaps those you don't like. Have a large rota placed in a prominent place so that each team member can see what their duties are and when. Larger STM teams are often split into group duties on a rotational basis, e.g. peeling the vegetables, washing up/cleaning the dishes, sweeping the yard, vacuuming the communal areas, doing the shopping at the local market etc. Depending on age, a leader may be assigned with each group or a local worker from the mission compound. You should not grumble and complain, but embrace the experience and get the victory. Do a good job as unto the Lord, even when you are not being watched.

The Bible states, 'As we have opportunity, let us do go good to all, but especially to those of the household of faith' (Galatians 6:10). Therefore we have an obligation to help and assist others, but especially the brethren, and as part of a STM team there will be plenty of opportunities for this. It could be: practical help in chores and duties, words of encouragement or in spiritual matters etc. But in our obligation lies a danger in which we may neglect an opportunity, thinking that someone else will do it. How many times have we left washing the dishes to another, yet we all ate at the meal table? Whilst others will try to justify their exemption from certain duties and being allergic to washing up liquid is a valid exemption, but that does not mean that they are exempt from laying the table, wiping up/drying the dishes and packing away or other important duties like peeling the potatoes or chopping vegetables!

Let us not be in the habit of making lame excuses to get out of practical chores, because we are only neglecting our duty and revealing to those around us our true character. If we 'love one another' as Christ commanded us to, we will want to help the team and function at our highest level.

Beware of:
- The dangers of familiarity as it can breed contempt.
- Doing the right things for the wrong motives.
- Being outwardly submissive but inwardly rebellious.
- Making promises that you have no intention of keeping.
- Deliberately rocking the boat so as to draw attention to yourself or playing the fool.
- Usurping authority or not being submissive to those who are over you.
- Breaking the rules – they are there for a reason.

More Effective than Defective
To be more effective than defective we need to lay aside our culture, our mindset and become servants, ready to serve; being clothed in humility and wrapped up in the love of Christ.
- Be prepared – spiritually, financially, physically and have the correct mentality – be positive.
- Be flexible – change happens, the best of plans can fall through.
- Be wise in all you do and say.
- Be kind and considerate to others.
- Wear the right clothing and be sensible.

- Have a willingness to learn and to be taught.
- When working with others, ask the right questions in the right way – inquire rather than condemn or accuse.
- Try to fit in – assimilate, mingle and interact (appropriately) with the locals.
- Be humble, gentle, kind, courteous and have a servant heart.
- Look after yourself, physically, spiritually, mentally and financially. It is easy to throw money into bottomless pits or to let one's self go when away from a familiar routine.
- Listen and obey your leaders – they will probably know best. They do not have to give the reason for their actions, requests or statements.

STM Frustrations and Inconvenience
- Pickpockets – those who steal from you.
- People who deliberately try and short-change you.
- People who blatantly lie to you and try to deceive you.
- When you are charged *a lot more* than the locals for goods or services because you are a foreigner.
- When you are asked for money, a tip (bakeesh in Egypt) or a gift, for no reason whatsoever.
- When a worker *demands* more money even though you have agreed a price with them beforehand. Even more so when the worker has not been helpful; you pay the agreed sum and then the worker gets angry and demands more, which you should not pay.
- People who try to renegotiate the cost of private transport when you're half way to your destination.
- Delayed transport (the ten hour train journey should have left at 6am but did not leave until 3pm!).
- Accommodation that has been pre-booked, but is not as described. It is a lot worse.
- Having to run around a capital city trying to obtain a visa, when the consulate only opens for one hour, two days a week. Dozens of people may be in the queue. (Sometimes you need proof of your onward travel before a visa is issued and/or a letter of invite from within that country).
- When a member of your team decides not to cooperate with the team or the leader.
- Your host regretting that he or she ever permitted the STM team to stay with him or her.

Chapter 21

Be Streetwise

'Only let your conduct be worthy of the Gospel of Christ, so that whether I come and see you or am absent, I may hear of your affairs, that you stand fast in one spirit, with one mind, striving together for the faith of the Gospel, and not in any way terrified by your adversaries...' (Philippians 1:27-28).

Entering into a new country you have to learn to be streetwise. If you are with an organization, stick close to your leader and keep an eye out for your fellow team members. Border crossings are the most wary places to be, but especially if you emerge from no-man's-land into a new country. In some countries, you cannot buy the next country's currency from a Bureau de Change or bank and so frequently have no option, but to buy money on the border. A slight-of-hand trick or a rigged calculator (so use your own) can cost you. Sometimes a zero or two is knocked off the end figure! Instead of getting 200,000, you may get 20,000! In some places there may be a black market, a better rate compared with the set rate of exchange. I have never used it, though many travellers have been exploited, even with out-of-circulation notes/bills or the money exchanger is an undercover police officer.

If you use facilities at a border town (e.g. a hotel), you need to know not only the cost, but clarify the currency as well. Don't assume prices are in the currency of the country you are in!

In many places of the world people *want* to carry your bags; it is unlikely that they will run off with a fully laden rucksack, but they *will* expect payment or take you to their preferred choice of bus, taxi, or hotel where you will end up indirectly paying for it. If you ask, "Where is the nearest hotel?" in developing countries some people will want to take you to it and expect financial recompense! Just ask to be pointed in the right direction. Others will take you to a hotel and ignore the guesthouse, hostel, B&B and other accommodation because you asked for *a hotel*. If they have gone out of their way then give them something for their time and don't let them run off with your wallet or purse! Keep some coins or small notes/bills handy.

I have found that in both Africa and Asia, children love to touch your skin, stroke your arms, and sometimes even adults, especially if you have hairs on them as Africans and Asians generally do not.

Africans are fascinated with straight soft hair, especially blonde-haired people, and do not be surprised if someone tries to stroke your hair or arms. Adults may ask, and it is nothing to be afraid of, but if you are a woman, be aware of men and rebuke them firmly if the occasion requires it! In China, many people wanted to take our photo, with them standing next to us – selfie! Others would try to do it discreetly, and we would stop and pose for them.

Christians in developing countries have informed me that in their nations, just walking alongside a foreigner bolsters their own status, but to talk with one is far better. These opportunities are always good to share the Gospel to those who have approached you, whilst some are best kept at arms length because you *know* they are up to no good as you feel uncomfortable in their presence. Others are just after a free meal, your contact details or will be friendly with you in an attempt to get closer to members of the opposite sex within the team. Always be ready to help a member of the STM team who may be pestered or harassed by a local – "We have to go, goodbye," and walk off together. A good test of the 'sincerity' of a local man speaking to a female member of your STM team is: Does he stay around when a male member of the team introduces himself and joins in the conversation?

Be aware of your surroundings. Be cautious who you go with or follow, if they have approached you, offering to show you something. They may lead you into a dark or quiet alley to rob you. Others may get you lost, and will *only* take you to your accommodation for a sum of money. Be shrewd in the discernment of people's motives. Your mission organization will advise you of no-go areas and places to avoid.

Sometimes you may take a person to a cafe to share the Good News with them and they will try to order everything! If they order a beer or cigarette, tell them that you will not be paying. A negative experience can still result in a positive testimony.

Getting Your Attention

In Africa to get your attention people will hiss as it is rude to shout, but in South-East Asia the customary, "You, YOU!" or "Oi!" yelled at the top of their lungs by a seller is common. Others try to get your attention by saying, "I want to show you something," or "I want to tell you something." You can be in the midst of a conversation and a person will interrupt, tug on your sleeve or even slap you gently on your arm to get your attention! There are those who want you to read out a printed letter on their behalf which is sometimes laminated, goes on to explain that this person, should be employed (as a guide or similar) with a recommendation from John Smith or Joe Bloggs, or that the person needs financial help. As much as these instances may be a nuisance, please remember that these types of people are only trying to make a living and the quality of your life compared to theirs is huge. If you were in their circumstances, you would probably do the same. Be polite and smile. Some sellers have some handy items, knickknacks or snacks (especially at bus stations) and you will be thankful that they approached you, whilst some guides are real gems of local knowledge and can take you into areas where you would have never trod.

Scams and Warnings

Additional food that you did not order can appear on your table and you will be charged for it, though in some places in North Africa, minted tea is freely served after the meal. Ask before you sip, otherwise it is too late and it goes on the bill! On rare occasions, bottled water can be delivered to your table and the seal may be broken. Always reject it, as it is but tap/faucet water at best or stream water at worse and could make you unwell.

Students who desire to practise their English may also approach you. A good opportunity to evangelise but be cautious if they invite you to a cafe or restaurant, as it may be their job to drum up customers into expensive establishments – such as happens in China. On the other hand, I have been in a restaurant having a meal with a group of local students and when the bill arrived, the locals vehemently complained to the owner over the inflated foreigner's bill!

Not everything that is labelled or touted as handmade is handmade. Just because someone puts a 'present' in your hand and tells you it's free does not mean that it will cost you nothing! At other times, sellers will put items in your hand and refuse to take it back, yet expect money for it. If you don't want the item and they refuse to take it from you then place it on the ground or somewhere safe and just walk away. Don't be emotionally manipulated into buying items you don't want or parting with more money than you want to.

Some calculators are set so as to deceive people. They can be known as trick calculators and are used by con artists, especially when calculating money in foreign exchange. For example, one calculator's total for 5 x 4 was not 20 but 16! To get this sum the owner pressed 5 x 4 x and the total would be 16 (notice the x sign). But if 5 x 4 = was pressed (notice the = sign) then the total would be 20. Take your own pocket calculator, it is essential.

Chapter 22

Spend Wisely

'His lord said to him, "Well done, good and faithful servant; you were faithful over a few things, I will make you ruler over many things. Enter into the joy of your lord" ' (Matthew 25:21).

You have saved for months, worked hard and been praying for the finances to come in and they did. So spend your short-term mission (STM) money wisely. Whilst the majority of this chapter is not relevant to those who are going with a mission organization, there are still helpful truths that will allow your money to go further and for you to be, hopefully, reducing the number of times you pay over the odds for items or services. Economising whilst on your STM can come in many shapes, sizes and varying ways and if you have learnt to economise at home then on your mission it will be just as easy, if not more. One of the best tips is to *always* ask the price before you agree to purchase; haggle and shop around for the best deal.

Many people automatically inflate the prices for foreigners so haggling is often essential. At other times, the cost of an item in the market or on the street may seem so reasonable that it is only fair to pay them what they ask without quibbling or haggling. Do not try to beat a market seller down by minute amounts when that extra will make all the difference to them and not to you. Have a conscience and use wisdom.

The price of a bottle of water and food can vary from one shop to the next. The amount of money saved may seem little, but over many months it adds up! The price may be printed on the product label but a shopkeeper may expect you to pay more. Point out the correct price. If they still disagree, go to another shop and pay the correct price.

If the seller begins to laugh once you have handed over the money, you know that you have paid over the odds. Pay a fair price for a fair product. If you have been financially exploited by a guide or tout etc. put it down to experience and learn from it.

Pre-Booking
Pre-booking tours or trains through an agent is more expensive than doing it yourself, but it does save time, though problems can be encountered. I rarely pre-book accommodation if just two people are

going (my friend and I), simply because four times out of five, I have experienced problems and once you are on the ground, you can see what is available and often get the best deal. Ask the locals.

Hotels, lodges and guesthouses often have star ratings and more often than not, the lower the star, the lower the price, though this is not always the case! In China (and once in Mongolia) we found the local hotels cheaper and much better equipped than the youth hostel or accommodation recommended by the guidebook. The advantage of an independent group is often purchasing power – you can go to a more upmarket hotel (e.g. 2 or 3 stars) during low season and pay the same as you would in one of a lesser quality (e.g. 1 or 2 stars). Often on STMs we ask the receptionist or manager if they have any cheaper rooms or if they can do a better deal. The worst they can say is no, and the best is a discount or an upgrade. The cost of accommodation varies greatly and most towns have several hotels or guesthouses, whereas some streets are full of them.

You can rent an apartment or large house for two weeks, a month or longer. Often this is easier with a person on the ground making the arrangements. High season is holiday/vacation season or at times of religious festivals and occasionally the demand can outstrip the supply, and that is when room prices/house rentals can be greatly inflated. You spend the same amount of money, but for less quality, you may get to share your room with cockroaches and other vermin!

An independent STM-er may stay in many different types of accommodation, such as a hotel, motel, youth hostel, lodge, inn, B&B, guesthouse, campsite or university accommodation (outside of term time, often in the summer). I do not recommend campsites on STMs because you have to take additional gear with you (tent and sleeping bag) and security is not great. For those frequently on the move, you may wish to purchase some address labels, instead of having to write your name and address every time you check-in.

How to Save Money

When it comes to your STM, there are many ways to save money, to stretch the team's budget – shop around for the best deals. The following are suggestions to consider.

- Go self-catering.
- Shop around for the best deals.
- As a team, negotiate a discount.
- Avoid the expensive hotel restaurant.
- Buy bread and fruit from the local market.
- Go to the local restaurant, cafe or street vendor.
- Rent or buy a local bicycle when you arrive.

- Take the bus instead of a taxi around town.
- Take a coach for longer distances instead of the train, as it is frequently cheaper.
- Travel overland across borders instead of flying. It takes longer, but you'll see more.
- The cost between hotels, inns, guesthouses, lodges, B&Bs, motels and hostels do vary.
- It is considerably cheaper to have two rooms with four people in each, rather than to have four rooms with two people in each. Is renting an apartment cheaper?
- Do I really need air-conditioning, a heater, a computer, a fridge or a TV in my hotel room?

Taxis and Transport

If you take a taxi use the meter (if it works) or agree on a price beforehand, if this is possible, otherwise any crazy figure could be given at the end of the journey. The danger with the meter is that you may be taken the long route. Some rickshaw drivers on arrival at your destination will ask (or even demand) more money than what you agreed before departing! Pay what you have agreed unless the 'driver' has been exceptionally helpful, then give a good tip, or if they have had to go out of their way, thus the journey took longer than anticipated.

Some countries have "skin tax" as one Asian pastor informed me whilst laughing profusely! On occasions, locals have arranged transport for us and bought the tickets on our behalf because they pay the going rate! Most guidebooks give approximate prices for various services and foreigners generally pay more than the locals.

Some taxi ranks are like bus stations where the 7-seat car or 10-seat minibus are lined up under different destinations, often competing owners. Many have workers whose job function is to direct you to where you need to go. They help fill up the vehicle so that it can depart when full and receive money from the company or driver.

Some taxis pick up people en route and in many African countries, this is common. Your agreed price may only include your seat (not the entire taxi) to your destination and a five-seat car may take six or seven passengers with two people on the front seat! It is common to be charged more than the locals. Sometimes they ask if you would like to pay for two seats, I never have.

In Tunisia, many taxis want to charge extra for your rucksacks or suitcases. In Nepal, sometimes the driver's friend will charge you for putting your rucksack on the roof, when all of the bags go on top and are tied down. Often they are covered with tarpaulin to keep the rain off and thieves away.

Long distance taxi drivers (which may be a minibus taxi) upon arriving in town will often drop people off at the depot/taxi rank or set stops or along a route. The driver may take you to a hotel, or a selection of hotels, but naturally, you will have to pay extra if this is out of the way. In Ethiopia, one conductor (money collector) walked us to the next taxi depot so we could catch a ride to the next town. In South Africa, one minibus taxi booked us on to two additional taxis (without our knowledge) because we wanted to travel to a particular city. We were not aware that the single taxi could not travel there in a single journey. After 16 hours or so of travel on three different minibuses it was great to arrive in Cape Town.

Taxi drivers often have the best local knowledge for cheap accommodation and you can save a small fortune. However, some taxi drivers or rickshaw drivers (notably in India) will take you to their preferred hotel (or shop) because they are paid to bring tourists there.

Be very wary if other people jump aboard your chartered transport, a vehicle and its driver which you have hired for the day, or just to a destination. Sometimes the driver brings his friends along for the ride (and you'll paying for it), whilst at other times they are there to back him up or are dropped off along route. If you are female then you should never travel without being accompanied by another woman and should refuse to go anywhere if men begin to pile in the back of the pickup or car which you have hired. With chartered transport pay on arrival, not before you depart, though sometimes petrol money may be needed to get you going. If so, you may (or may not) wish to give a percentage of the money before you drive off.

Souvenirs and Presents
- Do you really need to buy it?
- Haggle and do not pay more than what you want to.
- If you are buying a gift for your host, make sure the item has a function, and not a mantelpiece object.
- If you are buying gifts for your supporters back home, then make sure that they will fit into your rucksack or suitcase and travel well. Who wants to bring back a broken vase?
- Do not bring back false gods, tribal facemasks, and items connected with other religions etc., e.g. hand of Fatima earrings (Islamic), Shiva pendant (Hindu), Buddhist singing bowl, Zoroastrianism incense sticks, Aztec art or statues, New Age stones, or objects that are used in witchcraft/ occult rituals – they are accursed objects. See Exodus 20:3-6, Deuteronomy 7:26, 13:7, Joshua 6:18, chapter 7 and Isaiah 54:11. Some wood carvings may actually be

idols or representing spirit animals. Who or what do these items represent and what is the root origin behind them?

A False Economy

There is a time when economising to stretch your budget is a false economy. Eating street food can be one of the best culinary experiences on a STM; it is frequently cheap and fulfilling, but on occasions can make you unwell. Fresh fried food I have found to be the safest option, and I have always asked the vendor to put it back in the oil, or on the fire to burn off any germs as you don't know how long it has been sat around! Ask God to bless your food.

In the UK, I have never travelled first class on a train, but in developing countries I have. Sometimes it is worth paying more for peace of mind and added security whilst at other times it is merely foolish indulgence. In the case of train travel by night I have always paid the extra to have a bed and if possible a berth/compartment. At some ticket offices, it is assumed that you will have first class because you are a foreigner. For short journeys you may wish to travel 2nd or 3rd class. You can travel on a night bus or train, thus saving the cost of a room, but you may not get a good night's sleep.

Whilst God loves a generous giver; when you are travelling across a country on public transport, or taking frequent journeys every few days for months on end, then these savings do add up and you are able to be an extra blessing to your interpreter, the local church or individual brethren etc.

'The fear of the Lord is the beginning of wisdom; a good understanding have all those who do His commandments. His praise endures forever' (Psalm 111:10).

Tourist Sights and Attractions

Going on a short-term mission is not a holiday/vacation and should not be regarded as one. You are going there to work, to minister and to serve others. However, some organizations will take you to one or two places, not a theme park, but to sites of beauty or historical interest, to see a waterfall, gorge, old mission station etc. Some STM-ers disagree with this. As someone who appreciates history, who films for Christian television and writes Christian books, I believe that each mission should be rewarding; not only spiritual, but also educational, which is character building and stimulating. It adds to the experience and seeing important sights can help us understand the people and culture to whom we are ministering, or at least help us to understand to a small degree civilizations from the past.

Chapter 23

Security, Wisdom and Safety

Jesus said, "Behold, I send you out as sheep in the midst of wolves. Therefore be as wise as serpents and harmless as doves" (Matthew 10:16).

Wherever you go to in the world, even outside of your own front door you could encounter trouble, but wisdom and caution are the best line of defence; whether at home or on your short-term mission (STM). On rare occasions on STMs, countries (or some areas) can break out into political instability, so if you are an independent STM-er it pays to scan the local news headlines, international papers and look on your government's website as they issue travel warnings to its citizens. In many places of the world Westerners are targets.

Curiosity can override common sense, but avoid political rallies and demonstrations as they can turn nasty and you could end up in the middle of it. Tear gas, rubber bullets, and flying missiles (rocks and stones) make no distinction on whom they hit or affect. Keep away from drunken crowds.

Handbags and bum-bags (fanny packs/belt bags) are magnets for thieves. If you can loop your gadgets (e.g. digital camera or mobile/cell phone) on your belt covered by a long shirt or jumper (sweater) then this is better. Pockets with zips/zippers or velcro on trousers (pants) or skirts are very good for wallets, purses and passports. Some people have their passport and excess money in a pouch which is hung around the neck and tucked into one's top – out of sight, out of mind. Money belts are very good. Handbags can be easily snatched off the arm and can cause injury. Beware if people bump into you as they may be trying to steal from you, grope you, or coming between you as a group to pickpocket; or distracting you at a cafe, someone else takes your bag from under (or on top of) your table or chair etc. Hook your day-bag round your chair leg or through the arm of your chair.

It is unwise to invite a stranger into your hotel room as they may be a sex worker; regardless of the fact that they are the same sex as you. Most hotels do not permit room calls/visits because of this very problem. If you do invite a local back to your hotel and they are not a Christian worker then it is often best that they wait in the lobby area, as people do think the worst and you do not wish to give an 'appearance of evil' (1 Thessalonians 5:21), NIV, and not even a 'hint of sexual immorality' to be found among Christians (Ephesians 5:3), NIV. Your mission organization (or host) will have its own policy regarding visitors, find out what it is.

Don't invite trouble and be sensible in what you wear and where you go. It is always sensible not to go out alone in a foreign country, but even pairs and groups of foreign women will attract attention. It is always best for men to witness to men and women to witness to women, otherwise the one listening may have ulterior motives or you could get a bad reputation from the locals. Always let your team leader know where you are going and when you expect to be back.

As in your home country there are some places where it is advisable not to walk alone and not to go after dark. Unlit streets and alleyways are the norm in parts of the developing world and manhole covers may be nonexistent. Beware of potholes, raised kerbs, no sewer coverings, open sewers, ditches, uneven paving slabs and a thousand and one other obstacles in unlit areas.

God is sovereign – He is in control of all things and all things are under His control, but God's sovereignty does not relieve us of responsibility. We have common sense and it should be applied. We must look after ourselves and lookout for each other.

Problem People

Every once and a while I have encountered 'problem people' whilst on a STM and more often than not, it comes after something significant has happened. It is the devil's way of trying to frighten or discourage me, but these instances have only ever confirmed the good work that has happened. It may be the guy who is intoxicated or high on drugs; the criminal who is envious (or who despises your presence in their neighbourhood), those who are unbalanced in mind, the plain demoniacs and those in groups who are boisterous, being egged on by the crowd. In these circumstances, it is best to pray and walk away. In Dhaka, Bangladesh, due to an incident, we walked into a photographic shop and stayed inside until the crowd had dispersed.

> Jesus said, "...My friends, do not be afraid of those who kill the body, and after that have no more they can do. But I will show you whom you should fear. Fear Him who after He has killed, has power to cast into hell...fear Him!" (Luke 12:4-5).

Ignorance of the Law

There is a saying that goes, 'Ignorance of the law is no defence' and being in a different country than your own (with unfamiliar laws) does not mean that prosecution will be less swift if you break the law, nor will you have immunity because you are a foreigner. STM or no

STM, laws of the land have to be obeyed unless they break the higher law of God's decrees. Every form of wisdom and discretion should be used when you share the Good News or in the distribution of Christian literature etc. in sensitive countries, where it is illegal or discouraged to evangelise and/or proselytize (to change one's faith).

The laws of other lands, which may affect your STM, can range from no evangelising to the forbidding of distributing unauthorised literature. Most mission organizations stay on the right side of the law and would never intentionally put their STM-ers in danger or harms way, whilst those that do bend or flout the rules know the consequences and inform the participants of such.

Other laws which may differ from your own country can be: the forbidding of taking photographs of military installations or bridges, the forbidding of importing foods (or other), what you can wear, what you can say in public (religious or political, even comments on social media) or public interaction with members of the opposite sex (even when married). It may affect what you can take in (or out of a country), as well as various driving or travel regulations.

Political tension has revealed to the world the inflamed anger of some indigenous people in certain areas of a minority of countries. At other times, if you hold a certain passport, you may be denied a visa or forbidden access to enter a country, whilst a change of regime or government can change their ruling at a whim. In some countries, because of war, economic sanctions or the countries colonial past, some foreign citizens may face added danger (or disdain), thus hindering the work and possibly endangering those with them.

> "Did we not strictly command you not to teach in His name? And look, you have filled Jerusalem with your doctrine..." and Peter and the other apostles said, "We ought to obey God rather than men" (Acts 5:28-29).

Sensitive Countries and Christian Literature

Some STMs are based in sensitive countries where freedom of religion may not be permitted, even though a country's constitution may say otherwise, and so additional wisdom and caution is needed. If you are caught evangelising or distributing Christian literature you may be let off with a caution, (all your materials confiscated) or taken to the police station and interviewed, and then told to get on the next flight, or you might may have to appear in court. If you are permitted to leave the country those who have assisted you (or are associated with you, local Christians, the pastor, evangelist, interpreter or guide) may suffer the consequences. You need to seriously consider this before you enter a sensitive country.

Some items of literature are forbidden in sensitive countries, notably Christian pamphlets, gospels and Bibles, whilst in other countries, it is a crime to criticise the government or monarchy. Do not cause trouble or endanger the locals when giving them Christian materials, use wisdom for where and when you give out booklets, gospels, Christian DVDs etc. In one sensitive country we got caught giving out New Testaments (someone told the authorities, perhaps a recipient), but the policeman was delighted when he was offered one – and took it!

If a pair of team members (you work in twos) get caught by undercover police for giving out gospel booklets or New Testaments etc., go back to the hotel, (ask for the room key from reception) and empty their room of all Christian items. We did this once in North Africa and saved a married couple from a lot of trouble. The police entered their room with the couple, but it was the STM-ers who were most surprised, as all incriminating evidence had been moved into another room, and within hours, into another hotel.

The Last Word

Whilst we are to 'submit ourselves to every ordinance of man for the Lord's sake' (1 Peter 2:13-14), we also need to obey Jesus' command, "Go into all the world and preach the Gospel to every creature" (Mark 16:15). We know it is 'better to obey God rather than men' (Acts 5:29), therefore if the laws of the land contradict God's law (a higher law) then they can be broken, but we may have to face the consequences! As we could be sent out; to quote Jesus, "As sheep in the midst of wolves. Therefore be as wise as serpents and harmless as doves" (Matthew 10:16).

Paul Hattaway, Director of Asia Harvest wrote: 'Was Daniel misguided when he refused to obey the law of the land to bow before an idol? Were Peter and John sinning when they defied orders to stop telling people about Jesus? Peter and John replied, "Judge for yourselves whether it is right in God's sight to obey you rather than God. For we can not help speaking about what we have seen and heard" (Acts 4:19-20). I suspect many Christians today use the "obey the laws of the land" verse as a self-righteous excuse for doing nothing.'[1]

Do not disobey the rules of your mission or your host in his or her country. They know what is best for them, you and other STM-ers who will follow long after you have gone home.

Chapter 24

Look After Yourself

'Wisdom is the principle thing, therefore get wisdom. And in all your getting, get understanding. Exalt her, and she will promote you; she will bring you honour...embrace her' (Proverbs 4:7-8).

There are dangers and hazards everywhere, but on a short-term mission (STM) we should be extra diligent because of the unfamiliar surroundings, and heed any warnings that your mission organization or leaders inform you of. We should all be wary of extreme or adventure sports as an accident can spell the end of your STM. Each country may have its own unique difficulties that can cause problems, but these problems are a minority and incidences can be very few and far between. Leaders think on the following:

Whilst you are on your STM, you may have the opportunity to participate in a sport or activity, which may be a one-off opportunity. However, be aware that safety regulations and precautions may not be as stringent in some countries as in others – this is especially true in developing countries where corners may be cut to maximise profits. As a teenager I was a keen skateboarder and a lot more agile than I am now, I had bounce-ability falling over, now it is near breakability!

Travelling on public transport in some developing countries should carry its own health and safety warnings; where bald or under inflated tyres and worn brakes are common! As is overtaking on blind bends and weaving in and out of traffic, where the larger vehicles expect the smaller ones to give way. In Vietnam, before descending down a high mountain, the coach pulled over and the driver removed the wheels and checked the brakes. In northern Ethiopia, we saw many trucks and some coaches at the bottom of gorges! It appeared that most had gone over the edge on hairpin bends, unable to stop.

You can also fall off the back of a pickup, be bounced out of a truck or slide off the roof of a bus or a train and you would not be the first! What were you doing on the roof?

The human body can go through huge extremes and when in dire circumstances, with adrenaline flowing through its system, it can really go the distance, but only for so long until the body collapses. Food, drink and rest are essential, though within each of us we have greater endurance when pushed to extremes.

Don't forget your Sabbath day of rest, your one day off per week, which may not be a Sunday.

Most mission trips will run smoothly, though the more complex ones are when vast overland distances are travelled across different countries on public transport, working with different churches or Christian organizations.

The Power and Elements of Nature

It is very important not to underestimate the power and elements of nature. Whilst in some places the weather can be quite constant, in other places and especially at altitude or during certain seasons, the weather can turn on a knife-edge and temperatures can plummet rapidly. Rain and piercing wind can chill you to the bone within a short space of time, and is often not noticeable until you stop moving.

If you are going to be trekking into some remote area or jungle then glucose tablets for an instant energy boost will be beneficial, but most importantly *always* go prepared. Take fluids and food with you as well as adequate clothing. It is better that you have a little extra equipment than to be caught out. Trekking through jungles or in the wilderness can increase the strain on your mind and body, though the scenery can be outstanding.

Sunburn, sunstroke and heatstroke can all cause major problems on the mission field. The sun may be of much stronger intensity than what you are used to and relevant precautions should be taken. The sun is at its strongest from 11am-3pm. Slip on a shirt, slop on some suncream/sunscreen and slap on a hat. Sea and snow reflects and magnifies the sun's rays, and gives more exposure than if you were in the countryside or around town. Whilst you may not have had chapped lips at home, it is possible to get them abroad and in some climates, un-moisturised skin can quickly deteriorate and crack. Guys, remember that moisturiser and lip balm are not only for the girls.

Cloud cover does not eliminate harmful UV rays, especially in tropical climates and those countries centred near the equator. At the equator, with no previous exposure to the sun, the average person will begin to burn within fifteen minutes. Use a high factor suncream/sunscreen, especially on your arms, nose, the back of the neck and possibly even your earlobes. Just being outside whilst teaching, preaching, walking or working exposes you to UV rays, so look for shade or use an umbrella, cover up, wear a wide rimmed hat and drink plenty of fluids. Don't forget your sunglasses/shades.

The human body consists of between 45-65 percent water, depending on body size, age and gender. If you lose more than 5% of your body weight through loss of water, sweating, you will begin to deteriorate, physically and mentally. In hot climates you can lose 1 ½ litres/liters per hour and will need to drink up to ten litres/liters per day! If you lose just 2.5% of your overall bodily fluids (dehydration), then your efficiency to function decreases by a staggering 25%!

To minimise water loss, avoid talking and breathe through your nose. Ground temperature can be up to 30% higher than the surrounding air, so if you're in a jam and immobilised, then try to raise yourself off the ground onto a log, tree stump, or ledge and be in the shade. For the other extreme, you also do not want to freeze in artic temperatures so wrap up when the thermometer begins to plummet. In some desert areas, the difference between day and night temperatures can be a whopping 50ºC!

'Be anxious for nothing, but in everything by prayer and supplication, with thanksgiving, let your requests be made known to God; and the peace of God, which surpasses all understanding will guard your hearts and minds through Christ Jesus' (Philippians 4:6-7).

Animals, Insects, Bugs, Leeches and Mosquitoes

Each country has its own animals, insects, bugs, reptiles and rodents, some of which can cause harm. In many developing countries stray dogs can be a problem; but only if they bite you! A pastor in Sudan warned, "Throw stones at them to keep them away, they carry rabies." Take antihistamine tablets/cream to treat insect bits or skin rashes. The brand Sudocrem (in the UK) is a very effective antiseptic healing cream.

Leeches can be found in tropical locations or where damp leafy-type areas are humid. They can eat through clothes and will suck all the blood they can get from you, before falling off. Lighters are good for burning them to encourage them to drop off. Beware of squeezing them as you can push their bodily contents into your wound and this may lead to an infection.

Mosquitoes can be the bane of many a STM. I have never taken a mosquito net with me on any mission, though I have slept under dozens, but I have always bought anti-malarial drugs from home when going into an area of risk. Mosquito repellent containing DEET is essential and can be applied sparingly to exposed skin. DEET can irritate sensitive skin, especially on one's face. In Cairo, Egypt, I was bitten by a mosquito near my eye whilst sleeping. It swelled up, began to drag my upper cheek down and looked liked I had been punched in the face. It sorted itself out after three or four days.

Mosquito nets are useful if the place where you are staying in has the facilities to hang them! Nets that hang by one central cord are far better than those that hang by four corners; only one hook is needed rather than four. Mosquito nets are always cheaper in developing countries, though they may not have been sprayed or soaked in certain mosquito repellent liquids for additional protection.

Do not wear deodorant, perfume or aftershave in areas where malaria is common, because mosquitoes that transmit the disease are attracted by fragrance.

Be Watchful

On your STM you not only have to look after yourself, but you need to keep an eye on other members of the team, to consider their welfare and serve one another in the love of Christ. As a team member you are your 'brother's keeper' (Genesis 4:9), and are responsible to protect and watch over each other. This is why many mission organizations do not want you wandering around the streets on your own and why you should inform your leader where you are going, instead of playing the illusionist and disappearing!

Remember to assist those in need, be chivalrous (opening doors etc.), courteous and assist members of the team who are struggling to carry their bags, even though they should have travelled light.

'Commit your works to the Lord and your thoughts will be established' (Proverbs 16:3).

Unwanted Attention and Relationships

In some countries, foreign women can receive undue attention simply by their very presence in public. Headscarves and flowing tops often go a long way in some cultures to reduce unwanted attention. Some items of clothing and even jewellery can identify you with your religion, so beware of what you buy.

Mixed STM teams must use wisdom in how they interact with each other in public. Even married couples need to use discretion in public displays of affection, even holding hands in public in some cultures is a no-no! In the United Arab Emirates (UAE), kissing in public is deemed inappropriate behaviour with a possible prison sentence, penalty or deportation! Holding hands between unmarried couples is also inappropriate behaviour! For many years, Dubai in the UAE has been promoted as a holiday destination and is a short hop from Europe.

Some older unmarried female STM-ers have been known to wear a ring on their wedding finger, so as not to attract unwanted attention as they go about the work of the Lord, whilst unmarried men in certain environments arouse suspicion amongst the local males of the community.

If you are part of a mission organization, they will be able to advise you on all things cultural (and taboo), in regards to relationships.

They will probably have their own policy regarding starting a relationship with a member of the opposite sex and it will probably be "no;" or only with the leader's permission after a designated length of time.

It is advisable to refrain from getting emotionally involved with members of the opposite sex whilst on your STM; which includes those from within the team and members of the local community. These relationships will only distract you on your STM and can cause major problems if the relationship breaks down. You may still have two weeks (or two months) remaining of the STM, working in close proximity to the one who ended the relationship and it can cause friction for everyone. Also 'abstain from every form of evil' (1 Thessalonians 5:22). Remember that you are going on a STM to do the work of the Lord, not to get romantically entangled.

Narcotics, Stimuli and Other Substances
Be careful of what you are offered to chew or drink. If you are invited to smoke a substance, please decline. If you are offered a substance to chew (except chewing gum) then in all probability it will be a narcotic type stimulant. It may be perfectly legal and culturally acceptable, or perhaps even expected, but you should politely decline and stand firm. Other stimulants are snorted and any of the above, can really mess with your stomach and bowels, or head to produce a drug-like effect, hallucinations or even evil dreams.

All cultures have strange, weird, wonderful food and beverages, but some are not so good for you as others. You may not be teetotal, but on a STM I would advise to abstain from alcoholic drinks, though in France and Italy, it is the norm to have a glass of wine with your meal and the choice is always left up to the individual adult, unless it goes against the church or mission organization's rules. Do not lead young or weaker members of your team astray. In addition, there may be a former alcoholic on the team and your indiscretion could make them stumble. Use wisdom and refrain yourself. It is better to be safe than sorry. Some communion wine is alcoholic and that is generally permitted. However, if you are part of a mission organization or with the church, check with the leader.

The apostle Paul wrote: 'Let your conduct be worthy of the Gospel of Christ...' (Philippians 1:27a).

Chapter 25

Understanding Culture

'So they set him a place by himself, and them by themselves…the Egyptians could not eat food with the Hebrews, for that is an abomination to the Egyptians' (Genesis 43:32).

On your short-term mission (STM) outside of your own country or continent you can quickly discover that your concept of time and space differs, people dress and look differently, interaction with members of the opposite sex may be very different than what you are used to and values change.

Culture defines who you are, your social queues, familiar references and defines how things are done; because that is the way they have always been done. It is the way a group of inhabitants do things; their attitude, behaviour and values. Culture changes from people group to people group and from country to country. Culture can be broken into smaller segments within a country or even a county (or State) of how those in the north differ from those in the south, or east from west.

The culture of another can be simply observed from an outsider's perspective, but the closer you get the more complex it is! Culture within the same nationality can also change depending on one's upbringing or between generations.

The best way to see or observe culture is to go to an ethnic group other than your own; ideally, one that is outside of your own country. You will see the differences between yourself and them, and how you react to the way they do things or how they react to the way you do things! It is educational, funny, though sometimes an embarrassing experience, but a great learning curve, full of memories that can last a lifetime.

Every culture has its good and bad points, though ethnic members of each culture may not be able to see certain negative aspects until they are confronted with the culture of another. Culture is the norm of life, the way things are done and therefore each culture thinks that its understanding of the right, good and the true is best – if only because it has always been done that way. Other options may have never been considered or the tradition is just too strong to break. Some cultures do not use the Western idea of personal space or privacy and what may appear 'in your face' is normal behaviour to others.

Regardless of our nationality and cultural traits, we all need to be careful how we 'come across' when we interact with others, but as a STM team we must be aware that we do not present ourselves as loud and boisterous, especially on public transport and when in public places.

Culture Shock and Culture Fatigue

Arriving in any new destination on your STM can be a culture shock. It is often an immediate reaction when you pass through the airport doors onto the street or within a day or two when you venture out and about. It is when all your usual references have been taken away producing sensory overload and things can become a blur or a shock!

Your surroundings, the different language and culture, alongside different foods, temperature, and the spiritual atmosphere can all affect your mental wellbeing and spiritual perception, which can leave you feeling low or having a case of the blues.

As you begin to settle into a routine and the weeks or months pass by, you can begin to have culture fatigue, it happens over a period of time when you begin to get fed up with everything. You become tired, wearisome of your host, the people or your host country. You begin to criticize, complain, moan and whinge – "Why do they do it like this!?" You may feel frustrated over the language, troubled by the bland staple food or overpowered by the local spices, tired of the cold showers, lack of privacy, early mornings or late nights, the cold, humidity, heat, dirt floors, bugs, insects and flies, the inner city exhaust fumes, the people, the smells, anything and everything!

The disorientation of culture fatigue can manifest itself in many ways: stress and anxiety can make you feel less able to cope with your new surroundings and even minor incidents can seem like insurmountable hurdles. Stress can cause you to become irritable, angry, frustrated, tired and anxious and often leaves you unable to sleep soundly. '...Do not let the sun go down on your wrath, nor give place to the devil.' (Ephesians 4:26-27). Sometimes you can start to dislike the people you are ministering to, believing that your culture is right and that theirs is deeply flawed. You may start to resent your STM or even God Himself. You have to be very careful, as the devil will try to take full advantage of this (2 Corinthians 10:5). You may even resent the fact that you have to go home!

Where possible, talk the situation over privately with someone of your own nationality, a fellow worker, or your mission leader and talk to God about it. However, do not tell your host how much you dislike everything – that is not the answer, nor is posting your grievances on social networks! Most importantly, remember why you are on the mission (1 Timothy 1:12), trust in God and remember to pray for love, grace and strength.

There are also some practical remedies to help combat culture fatigue. Relax and if possible, with your leader's permission, take some time out, as you may be over-doing it. Appreciate the beauty of your surroundings and do some exercise, as it is good to get the body moving. Catch up on lost sleep and missed meals. Go to bed earlier, and you should not be too busy to eat. Daily, ask God for His grace. Sometimes we can be caught in the rut of a STM (just like in a 9-5 job) where everything seems the same, as every other day and sometimes we all need a new challenge, which can help us refocus our efforts. Culture shock or culture fatigue does not affect all people – some people are not fazed by anything!

You may encounter culture confusion where you can see the good points in your host's culture and the weaknesses in your own (and vice versa) and have trouble trying to reconcile two cultures into one. It can be like standing at a set of crossroads unsure of where to go and not knowing which direction to take or how best to go about it.

Christian Culture Versus Non-Christian Culture

When missionaries first took the Gospel into various lands they had to sift through the local culture to see what was compatible with Christianity, what was not, what could be retained, and what had to go upon profession of conversion. Various cultural ways can be compatible with the Bible, but also at odds with it and on your STM you may run into this:

1. It is compatible, if it is a biblical principle.
2. It is incompatible, if it is unbiblical.
3. It is neutral and can be retained.

Exporting Christian Culture

We need to be careful that on our STM we are not exporting *our* Christian culture or the culture of *our* denomination and trying to implant it or *force* it on the Christian culture of another. This is true if we are part of a mission organization, going with our church or if we go with a friend or group of friends as independent STM-ers. Beware of your preconceived ideas, interpretations and opinions or prejudice (nationalistic, personal, racial, theological and denominational), which can distort biblical doctrine.

Church members often think that what they do on a Sunday morning is pure Christian culture whereas it may only be British, American (or Western) Church culture – it is the way we do things and our interpretation of certain Scriptures coupled with tradition. Often our opinions are formed more by our country or denomination's traditions rather than what is laid down in the Bible.

Are our Christian practices biblical or cultural? To answer this we each need to read the Bible and see if what we do is in line with Scripture.

Biblical Christianity must be allowed to blossom and flourish within its own setting. On our STM we should export the Christ of Christianity and not *our* culture of Christianity – but we should live the culture of Christ – to love one another and to serve others.

Wherever you go and whatever you do on your STM, you must serve the people in humility and love, and remember that what works in one community (or on one STM) may not work in another. For experienced and mature STM-ers who go to plant or establish a new church, they will know that it is best not to fit the national converts into the mould/mold of their home culture. Styles and formats may need to be altered to adapt to the country they are in when forming a church, which identifies with the people group they are working with. This will help put seekers at ease and aid evangelism.

John Wimber wrote: 'From earliest childhood, Western people are trained in deductive reasoning; we draw conclusions based on rules of logic to guide our lives. The presuppositions of our society encourage us to think this way. The assumptions of most Eastern, African and South American societies do not. Their people think more concretely and pictorially. The exception to this is found among those with Western schooling. (I am not implying that our society is superior to the others, only that it is different).'[1]

Missionary to Namibia, Janny van der Kliss wrote: 'We all have a personal grid through which messages of non-verbal nature pass and by means of which we understand their meanings.'[2]

Culturally Sensitive – the Church and Traditions

Being culturally sensitive also borders between Christian communities and what is acceptable in one church or Christian culture in one setting may be frowned upon in another. In some churches, men sit on one side and women on the other; in some denominations, children and/or teenagers participating in communion is forbidden and how church services are structured vary.

Other cultural factors can be:
- The consumption and use of tobacco.
- The wearing of earrings, nose studs and flesh tunnels.
- Tattoos (can they be covered up?) and nose bones.
- Other body piercings and jewellery (even crosses).
- Type, style and cut of clothes – what is acceptable and what is not – is it too revealing or too tight?
- Long hair versus short hair (for both men and women).

- Makeup and nail varnish (even on your toes).
- Unnatural hair colouring (pink, green or blue etc.).
- Mixed bathing (in swimming baths, lakes or in the sea).
- Types of swim wear – is it modest?

On your STM be culturally sensitive to those around you and that includes the brethren, and even if eating meat causes a brother to stumble, we should not eat it (1 Corinthians 8:12-13).

Worship – in the East, people take off their shoes, but in the West, they take off their hats. However, in a synagogue you must wear a covering for your head.

'Love suffers long and is kind; love does not envy; love does not parade itself, is not puffed up; does not behave rudely, does not seek its own, is not provoked, thinks no evil; does not rejoice in iniquity, but rejoices in the truth; bears all things, believes all things, hopes all things, endures all things' (1 Corinthians 13:4-7).

Earrings, Piercings, Cuttings and Tattoos

Earrings and body piercings can be very problematic, but especially for men. In some countries, it is a cardinal sin for a man to have an earring (Romania) and in others, even among women it is frowned upon. You may be the youth leader, or the team's greatest evangelist, but your fashion or style statement may bring your words to deaf ears and only distance or alienate yourself (and possibly your team) towards those you are trying to reach or those you work with.

Tattoos/inking can also be problematic. You can wear long sleeves or long trousers to cover up. In the Arab world and in Hindu custom, henna tattoos are part of culture, religion and ceremonies, where different patterns on various parts of the body represent or announce certain things. Henna tattoos are non-permanent and last several weeks.

Tattoos, flesh piercings, flesh tunnels and cuttings (mutilation/self-harm) in the Scriptures are linked with men involved in occult practice and devotion to the dead! See 1 Kings 18:22-28, Jeremiah 16:6, Mark 5:1-5 and Leviticus 21:5 and Deuteronomy 14:1-2. It is revealing that the Scriptures foretell that in the end times the Beast will mark his own! See Revelation 13:16-18, Revelation 14:9-11, Revelation 16:1-2 and Revelation 19:20-21. In some countries, the host you are working with, or the local Christians, may want to know why members of your STM team have gone back to their ancestral tribal past with body piercings, flesh tunnels and tattoos (Leviticus 19:28 and 1 Corinthians 6:19-20), which the missionaries told them to give up because of their roots in pagan culture and practice!

Chapter 26

Being Culturally Sensitive

'Give no offence, either to the Jews or to the Greeks or to the church of God, just as I also please all men in all things, not seeking my own profit, but the profit of many that they may be saved' (1 Corinthians 10:32-33).

The people we meet on our short-term mission (STM) will be different than ourselves, in a similar way that we are different to them. Understanding culture can be complex and to an outsider, some customs, rites or just the way things are done may seem absurd. Nevertheless, if we want to go from an outsider to an insider we have to try to adapt; to do things the local way thus making it easier to be accepted into the society we are trying to serve and reach. We do not enter into the culture of another to judge them (or condemn them), but to serve them and to reveal the love of Christ through our words, lives and actions, and we certainly cannot demand or expect them to enter into our culture with all its flaws and weaknesses.

When sharing the Gospel be careful not to wrap the Good News in Western Christian verbiage/phraseology, words like: 'justified,' (Romans 3:24 and Galatians 2:16), 'sanctified' (1 Corinthians 6:11 and Jude 1:1), and 'washed in the blood' (Revelation 1:5). These phrases may be common to Christians, but will mean little to nothing to those from a non-Christian heritage. These words may be difficult to interpret (unless the interpreter is familiar with the particular Scripture in your language), or be interpreted literally – 'washed in the blood,' and stun an individual or an audience!

Culturally Sensitive

Being culturally sensitive means that we should be aware of the basic cultural do's, or more importantly, the don'ts (cultural faux pas – a slip up), and where possible find out the taboos – what to avoid, what not to discuss and abide by them! Nobody expects you to be an expert on all things cultural, but a few essential basics are well – essential! The locals will more than likely chuckle by minor misdemeanours, but may not be so forgiving on major issues of culture, especially in the context of relationships and religion.

Be cautious how you interact with members of the opposite sex; even those at church. You may be accustomed to giving strangers big warm hugs (or air kisses) as part of your introduction/greetings, but at times, it would be more appropriate to smile, say hello and just put out your hand, though in some places even this is a step too far! Being too friendly in some cultures is an indication of wanting to have a sexual relationship with them!

For younger STM-ers avoid talking about your *own* room, your computer, TV, smartphone, pocket money or perhaps even your pet horse. Team leaders and older STM-ers, do not discuss your house, your car(s), holidays/vacations, Christmas bonus, your investments or the stock market (how much you've made or lost). What you earn in a day may take a month of hard labour for your host; don't be insensitive. Your host may struggle to give two nutritious meals to their children a day.

In the Arab world, a dog is unclean, in the West it is a pet, a guard dog, or a guide dog, whereas in Korea it is a delicacy, though some Koreans do keep them as pets. In many parts of the world, a horse is a work-animal, for pulling carts, carrying loads or a means of transport, in France it is also food. Showing a picture to your Arab host (or the Arab you are trying to reach out to), of you and Lassie embracing as 'man's best friend,' will not help you become friends! Hindus, Muslims and Jews are all forbidden by their religion to eat pork. Stay clear of bacon and Hawaiian pizza if in their presence.

> 'We give no offence in anything, that our ministry may not be blamed' (2 Corinthians 6:3).

Mannerism and Gestures

Be careful of your mannerism and gestures, as body signals mean different things around the world. If you're in Brazil and give the thumbs up sign 'its OK, it's good,' it means you want to have sex! In Hindu and Muslim cultures, the left hand is considered unclean, so be careful what you touch and do not eat with your left hand! But how do you hold your veggie burger? In the Middle East, crossing your legs and showing the soles of your feet is disrespectful. Be very careful (wherever you are) with eye contact with the opposite sex, and how you greet them (if at all). A Western glance in an Eastern setting may be taboo!

Customs and Culture

A Ghanaian proverb states: 'Rather let your children starve than have a guest go hungry.' In Western culture, this proverb is difficult to fathom in practice, but it brings to light the importance of hospitality. In the West we put our aged parents in nursing homes, whereas in many cultures to pass over the responsibility of those who brought us into the world and took care of us as a child is considered wrong. A number of cultures have more than a nuclear family (parents and children) living under the same roof, often it is three generations.

In American culture, to say, "Thank you" to someone who has helped or served you requires a response, often, "You're welcome." I have also heard this response in a few Asian countries. To say that a place is "homely" in America will be received as an insult (this place is plain or ugly), but a complement in Britain (this place is cosy)! In America, the word homey is preferable however with pronunciation and accents you may make a faux pas and get it wrong! The phrase 'wash up' in Britain means to 'clean the dishes' however to 'wash up' in America means 'go wash your hands' – the meal is about to be served. To 'crack a window' in America means to open it a little, not to damage it!

Superiority, Pride, Prejudices and Racism

Superiority and pride has no place in Christendom, let alone on STMs and if you have issues in these areas you must deal with them before you depart. Looking down upon anyone is a sin and must not be entertained.

On the mission field of your STM, many minor things may annoy you; don't let it get you down. If things are going hard, the enemy may tell you that you are from the *West* and they are from the *third-world* and thus try to make you feel better by having an attitude of superiority, enabling you to rise above your discouragements by putting others down. This is exactly what a school bully does, he or she puts others down to raise their own self-esteem. It is sin.

It is not uncommon for humans to laugh at, or at worst, look down upon others who cannot perform or do what is second nature to us. In the West, the vast majority of people can set a washing machine, surf the internet, turn on the DVD recorder (or HD TV box), or use a smartphone etc., but often if we go to a developing country, we can be like fish out of water. What is normal to one community can be seen as an unusual custom for another. Foreigners in a developing country are often deemed 'uneducated' because they do not have the basic life-skills of cultivating and tilling the ground or knowledge of how to pluck, gut and cook a chicken.

Racism and prejudice are sin, and preconceptions can be much farther from the truth than what we had once believed and cross the sin boundary when we judge another. Anyone of us could have been born in a different country and into a culture where education and the social or political sphere could have been very different than our present one.

As you travel to different locations you may see some weird, wonderful and wicked (evil and terrible) sights, but the minority of a few, or the occasional negative incident should not be allowed to dim the light of your STM. It could be said, "There go I bar the grace of God."

Georgina Gollock wrote: 'Never trifle with a *conviction*, but be utterly merciless to a *prejudice* – if it is your own! These painful prejudices are the cause of half the difficulties in Christian work and the man who is in the habit of yielding to prejudices is sure to cause sorrow to others and to himself.'[1]

Personal Hygiene and Water Safety

Personal hygiene varies from one person to another, but in regards to areas and nationalities, they are generally uniform. In many developing countries of the world, the priority is to get food on the table and everything else takes second place, even purchasing soap. Deodorants are available in developing countries, especially in the capitals, though their prices are often the same as in the West, which for many nationals is too expensive. Whilst you may meet people who smell, it is more often than not because they have done a hard day's work and have yet to return home and wash. In some countries, water is precious and having enough for the family and their herd is the top priority, whilst tens of millions of homes do not have running water. Washing can be a luxury, though we must be careful to maintain our personal hygiene on our STM.

I have always taken a can of deodorant with me whilst on a mission and when it runs out, it runs out and I only replace it a few weeks before I depart for home – I do not want to smell on the plane! Remember: deodorant cans cannot be taken on a plane as hand/carry-on luggage, so spray up before departure. Whilst virtually everyday I have been able to take a shower or at least wash in a bowl. Some countries are so hot and humid that after you have dried yourself, you begin to perspire again. In areas where malaria is common, mosquitoes that transmit the disease are attracted by fragrance e.g. perfume, aftershave or deodorant.

In some areas, the river may be the place where you wash yourself and your clothes. Locals often do a far better job at washing clothes (and a lot quicker) and are happy for the extra income. If you have to wash in a river, ask the locals to find out where the best place is and what is the best time.

At certain times of day, animals may come to feed or be watered! The locals may not appreciate your soap or washing suds polluting their drinking water. Find out what creatures lurk in the river – crocodiles, hippos, piranhas etc! If there are crocodiles, do not collect water from the same place everyday. Beware of jellyfish!

Sometimes waterborne diseases or micro-organisms can be present which can infect you. Common sense goes a long way, but a simple question to a local can be returned by a simple answer, thus alleviating yourself of any fears or concerns that you may have.

Can you Give Me?

Wherever you go on your STM people will ask for your telephone number, address, email, social media details or possibly letters of introduction and invites. Sometimes the latter requests come after you have arrived home or have corresponded for a few months. Some requests come from complete strangers, would you give your telephone number and address to a person you sat next to on the New York Metro or London Underground?

I have also found in some places it is best not to reveal where you are staying, in which hotel or guest house etc., just be vague. In one town in Kenya, a man tried to enter our hotel claiming to be our friend (presumably to get access to our room). The security guard was wise enough to remove him from the hotel and reported the incident to us. We had only arrived the day before, only spoken to a few people, and told no one where we were staying.

Some people you meet on STMs are *only* out to get what they can from you, whilst others need genuine help. Some think that you are rich (because you have flown to their country or are far from home), they only have to ask, after all, the worst you can say is no. You may be more financially secure than many people you meet, but many people will have their own land and home, which makes them wealthier than the average young STM-er who lives with their parents or who still has a mortgage on their home.

For non-Christians whom I have shared the Good News with, I have always given them my secondary email address if they have asked to keep in touch. Since the advent of widespread internet, I have never given out my home address. A foreign address can be a valuable asset to a scheming person, as one day you may find uninvited visitors, 'friends of a friend' on your doorstep, relating to the person you met on a STM. They have just arrived and have no place to stay, and no money! This is an extreme example, but not unknown!

Chapter 27

Culinary Delights and the Tribe

'Whether you eat or drink or whatever you do, do all for the glory of God. Give no offence, either to the Jews or to the Greeks or to the church of God' (1 Corinthians 10:31-32).

The world has much to offer in the realm of culinary delight. If you are with a mission organization you will be well looked after, hopefully, but it may take time for your taste buds to adapt! On your short-term mission (STM) you rarely have to go without, unless you live frugally which is often a false economy. When I first went to India, I really wanted a cheese and pickle sandwich, but could not get one!

The global market has much to offer and on STMs it is always interesting to try different foods. You may encounter on your local menu, the familiar and unfamiliar! For many, it will be a time to say 'grace' with faith, rather than by repetition, and remember to have water handy to 'wash it down' or to douse the hot spices! An old missionary creed states: 'Where He leads me I will follow. What they feed me I will swallow!'

In most major cities, there may be familiar fast food chains, or a local imitation, which you may not appreciate! Some countries' carnivorous food may well be a pet from home. In the West, we go to the supermarket (or order online) and have a sanitised view of pre-packaged meat, whereas in much of the developing world, you go to the market, buy your meat fresh (e.g. chicken), kill it and prepare it.

Hygiene, refrigeration and pasteurisation may not be as good as at home. This means that some foods/drinks or at certain times of the year (especially when hot) may make you unwell. Raw meat and fish, cream, mayonnaise and cooked food that has been left around in humid temperatures can make you ill. Even salads, fruit and vegetables washed in local water may be problematic. One saying is: 'Boil it, cook it, peel it or forget it,' but this is not always practical or possible. A distinction should be made for those who are going on a STM for two weeks or three months. You cannot avoid most types of food your entire STM, but you do not want to be ill for a week when your STM is only two weeks in duration! For longer STMs, you can try eating small amounts of different types of food, or taking a sip of the local water, to see how it affects you and to help build up your immune system. It may not be the food that is the problem, but the restaurant where it is prepared and sold. Self-catering STM teams can wash vegetables, fruit and salad items in water with chlorine or iodine to help kill germs. Frying food in very hot oil helps kill germs.

'For the Kingdom of God is not food and drink, but righteousness and peace and joy in the Holy Spirit' (Romans 14:17).

Food Etiquette and Vegetarian Meals

In many countries, you *only* eat with your right hand. Trying to separate meat with only one hand and no utensils is a real bind and tricky, that is why in Japan, meat is cut into portions to enable you to pick them up with your chopsticks. Your eating utensils and accompanying food 'plate' could be: A knife and fork, spoon, chopsticks or by hand. Your food could be placed on a paper, plastic, wooden or ceramic plate, or saucepan lid; served on the table, on a banana leaf or in old newspaper.

You (and your team) may be invited into a home as the guest of honour, what they set before you may be a much larger portion than what they serve themselves, or an expensive speciality food. To refuse may be seen as an insult, whereas at other times, if you eat it all, you could be deemed greedy! You may get first pick of the bowl and when you have eaten, the host (and/or their children) will be permitted to tuck in. Remember, in many cultures it is customary to bring a gift for your host or when invited to a home for a meal.

Being a vegetarian by choice is not the norm in most countries and in places where you can buy vegetarian dishes it may not be vegetarian enough! Encountering indigenous 'vegetarians' is often because they are too poor to eat meat, or because of religious reasons (e.g. India or Nepal). I ordered a vegetarian curry in Ulaanbaatar, Mongolia and the server asked if I was a vegetarian. I said, "No." The curry that was put before me had several tasty lumps of tender beef with freshly cut chunks of carrots!

To burp in India after a meal is considered a compliment, but not in Britain where it is rude, as is blowing your nose at the meal table in Korea. In some cultures, you leave some food on the plate as a sign you're full, at other times you eat it all! In some cultures you accept a little food, move it around your plate and it's OK, in other places it would be frowned upon as playing with your food. Sometimes refusing a drink is rude (a non-alcoholic drink), but you can accept it, put it to your lips, without drinking any and then place it on the floor or table without offending your host. Watch and observe the locals who are always forgiving towards foreigners and will more often than not, if you get it wrong, laugh at you, rather than rebuke you – it is good practice to laugh with them.

Whatever is put before you partake of it (unless your conscience says otherwise), regardless of how unpalatable it looks, imagine it is your favourite food, be positive. Try to be thankful and grateful, and look as if you are enjoying it. Jesus said to the seventy whom He sent out in pairs on their STMs, "Whatever city you enter, and they receive you, *eat such things as are set before you*" (Luke 10:8). The apostle Paul wrote to Timothy: 'For every creature of God is good, and *nothing is to be refused if it is received with thanksgiving*; for it is sanctified by the Word of God and prayer' (1 Timothy 4:4-5).

Free WiFi at Cafes or Restaurants

When I first went on a STM as a teenager there was no such thing as the internet or mobile/cell phones! In 2011, I purchased a Mini laptop with a 10-inch screen, WiFi enabled with 6hrs battery life specifically for a 3 ½ month STM in Asia. (You may prefer a Tablet, iPad or smartphone). Many countries have free WiFi hotspots and it was the first time on a STM that I did not have to pay to use the internet! Some hotels have internet cables in their rooms or in their lounge or lobby area, which you can plug into your laptop. Other establishments advertise their free WiFi zone within their cafe, restaurant or museum. However, they do not always work, or the staff are unsure of the network or password. Check that the WiFi works before you order a drink or a meal! Li-Fi, a light-based data delivery method may replace WiFi in the future.

You may be able to let your friends and followers know of your mission via social networking sites or micro-blogs subject to your team leader's approval, but NOT in sensitive countries. Remember, sometimes non-Christian 'friends' will be viewing your updates (your old school buddies or work colleagues) and this could have a detrimental effect as they may speak negatively about your work. Beware that social networking sites do not become your master and you become its slave.

Helpful Hints, Tips and Advice

Within the remainder of this chapter is a collection of incidences and a compendium of helpful hints, tips and advice. For ninety-five percent of those going on a STM, virtually none of the things within this chapter will affect you and is confined to isolated tribes or to some degree, communities that are way off the standard mission group trail; though the declaration at the end of the chapter is very important. These tips and advice are included because you never know what is around the corner or where you may end up, as the twists and turns in the sovereignty of God may lead you into deeper areas of work in the coming years.

The type of independent missions that take you to isolated areas or remote tribes cost considerably more than your average trip with any mission organization, though you can tie up with specialist agencies and Christian NGOs (non-governmental organizations). The tribes are isolated in their locations, and often 4x4s or boats and motorised canoes have to be hired or rented, along with their driver/captain, as well as a interpreter/guide. To protect your ears from noisy engines, use ear plugs or roll up tissue paper and place inside your ears! You will need to kit yourselves out with enough camping gear for the entire team and food to last you (and your helpers) the duration of the mission, as well as spares and fuel. Everything adds up. Also remember that "white man's" diseases can easily wipe out an entire tribe who have not had inoculations or vaccinations which are common to those of us in the West.

In some places, it is customary to bring presents to those who are in charge or to bring assistance to their people. Staple foods, pots and pans, matches or disposable lighters, knives, machetes, axes, clothes, blankets; really anything to help open the minds of those you are trying to reach and thus open doors. Your guide and interpreter are always your best port of call for advice in these matters and they will probably understand the culture, customs and etiquette.

One STM team were visiting an Amazonian tribe. The leader said, "They don't want any books, if they have time to read they have time to hunt! Leave them behind." In some remote locations, you and your baggage will be weighed to make sure the plane can clear the trees at the end of the runway! Please note, some tribes would rather have your friendship than for the team to build them a house or church building.

In some places, before you can camp in a village or interact with the locals, let alone share the Good News, you will have to speak to the chief, village elders or patriarchal figure. Your guide or interpreter will assist you in this cultural issue. With those in charge on your side, your ministry in that location can begin.

If you are unable to obtain the consent of the chief, then generally speaking, the villagers will be afraid to go against the express wishes of their superior. It is often better just to move on whilst still in the patriarchal's good will, rather than to offend. The leader may only be distrusting because it is the first time he has laid eyes on you. It may be possible to visit at another time, on a return trip and the door may be wide open. Sometimes the cultural etiquette is to bring gifts for the chief, village elders or for the village at large, often for the heads of families.

Superstition, Witch Doctors and Declarations

Do not underestimate the power of superstition and the control and fear which witchdoctors or shamans can hold over their people. Whilst these workers of unrighteousness are demonised, only a minority have real power, which comes from the evil one; many are just charlatans. Never forget that 'He who is in you is greater than he who is in the world' (1 John 4:4), and that Jesus was 'manifest that He might destroy the works of the evil one' (1 John 3:8). If you come across these workers of unrighteousness and bond-slaves to the devil, they may challenge you, or more often than not, try to conjure enchantments or cast spells against you, perceiving that you are servants of the living God. If you are born again and not living in wilful sin you have nothing to be afraid of, as you are covered by the blood of Christ and there is no greater name than Jesus Christ of Nazareth!

'Whoever is born of God does not sin; but he who has been born of God keeps himself and the wicked one does not touch him' (1 John 5:18). The devil always stands to accuse, but the innocent who are washed in the blood of the Lamb can declare, "The Lord rebuke you Satan" (Zechariah 3:1-5), because our 'Advocate,' Jesus Christ 'is the propitiation for our sins' (1 John 2:1-2).

Much of what happens in this world goes on in the unseen realms and the 'whole world lies under the sway of the evil one' (1 John 5:19), as the thief has come only 'to steal and to kill and to destroy' (John 10:10). The apostle Paul wrote: 'We do not wrestle against flesh and blood [humans], but against principalities, against powers, against the rulers of darkness of this age, against spiritual hosts of wickedness in the heavenly places' (Ephesians 6:12). This is why we must have on the 'whole armour of God' (another declaration and prayer, see Ephesians 6:10-17), and be 'praying always with all prayer and supplications in the Spirit, being watchful to this end with all perseverance...' (Ephesians 6:13-18).

You should try to memorise some of the above Scriptures and proclaim Jesus Christ's victory – that Jesus is Lord, the Victorious Conqueror, that Jesus is the name that is above all others and that He defeated the devil. It is also important to plead the protection of the blood of the Lord Jesus Christ over your life – and declare that 'no weapon formed against you shall prosper...' (Isaiah 54:17).

These truths are declarations and should come from the heart, they are not mantras. It is very important that you are not living in deliberate sin, that you keep a short account with God and your fellow team members (repent and ask forgiveness when you sin), working in unity, with one mind, for the glory of Jesus Christ.[1]

Chapter 28

A United Front

'Let nothing be done through selfish ambition or conceit, but in lowliness of mind let each other esteem others better than himself. Let each of you look out not only for his own interests, but also for the interests of others' (Philippians 2:3-4).

The leader(s) of a short-term mission (STM) team have the most demanding roles. They make the final decisions and have a whole host of other responsibilities to deal with, which includes keeping an eye on every member of the team, mediating between the host church, community or local missionary, the logistics of travel; seeing that everything goes as smoothly as can be expected, as well as "rallying the troops" into action.

During your STM, the team should meet for prayer, short Bible study and worship once a day. There should also be an opportunity for people to talk, share their concerns and for the leader(s) to keep the team up-to-date. Leaders have to deal with not only people and their successes, but their personalities and their problems, and to keep the STM team focused on its aims and goals.

Within any group of people there will be differences and stronger characters will come to the fore. Within your STM team there should be the greatest of cooperation, but it is inevitable that problems will arise. Your fellow team members on your STM may have just as many problems as yourself and so conflict and tension can arise. There may be many underlying issues that affect individuals, as well as their gender, age, level of maturity and preconceived ideas. Jesus said, "...Love one another; as I have loved you... By this all will know that you are My disciples, if you love one another" (John 13:34-35). Leonard Moules, a missionary field leader in the Himalayas noted that in the wisdom of God's sovereignty, we are often placed alongside the most uncongenial members because God has a work in us to do! In relation to difficult colleagues, Len noted that there are three courses of action open to us:

1. We can avoid them like the plague – with the least contact the least provocation!

2. We can grit our teeth and pray for grace to grease the friction points!

3. We can see in the other person the graces and gifts of God we each so sorely need to enrich our lives.[1]

Community is the place where the person you least want to live with, always lives – Henri Nouwen.

Contentions with the Team

Try to be Christ like in all you say and do, remembering to be kind, courteous, respectful, gracious, forgiving and loving. Treat others how you would like to be treated. The apostle Paul wrote that the team that worked alongside him at Thessalonica laboured night and day so they 'might not be a burden to any' (1 Thessalonians 2:9). Whilst he was writing in the context of finances, let us not be a burden to our leaders or to other members of the team.

- 'The beginning of strife is like releasing water; therefore stop contentions before a quarrel starts' (Proverbs 17:14).
- 'He who has knowledge spares his words and a man of understanding is of a calm spirit. Even a fool is considered wise when he holds his peace; when he shuts his lips, he is considered perceptive' (Proverbs 17:27-28).
- 'Let us pursue the things which make for peace and the things by which we may edify another' (Romans 14:19).

'...Recognise those who labour among you, and are over you in the Lord and admonish you, and to esteem them very highly in love for their work's sake. Be at peace amongst yourselves' (1 Thessalonians 5:12-13).

Duty and Responsibility

Many STM-ers may be used to having everything done for them. At a set time everyday, meals appear on the table; dirty washing is thrown into a basket and within a few days it reappears clean and ironed! A mess is made in the bedroom, yet every week the room is dusted and vacuumed. On the mission field, there is no Mum/Mom and each individual has to take responsibility for themselves, but please help the not so adept members of the team.

Defiance of rules can lead to open opposition, whether it is the rules of the nation or the rules of a mission organization. Policies are frequently laid down because mission organizations who have put them in print have learnt from experience. Remember that it is possible not the break the letter of the law, but the spirit behind it. Don't be a rebel and look for loopholes!

Within any team there are many different responsibilities and functions. If members of a sports team decided to do their own thing then the team would not function at its best. If this happens within a STM team, the consequences will be bad at best and disastrous at worse. Each member of the STM must be a team player, because: 'A man who isolates himself seeks his own desire; he rages against all wise judgment' (Proverbs 18:1). Remember, Jesus sent the twelve disciples and the seventy out in pairs – team work!

We must also be aware that we can listen but not hear, and look but not see. We can nod our head, but not understand; think we understand yet not comprehend. Often we have to read between the lines when we are communicating with others, and in another culture, that is even harder than at home.

What to Do

- Serve others.
- Be kind and gentle.
- Learn some local phrases.
- Honour people and walk in humility.
- Be considerate of others (especially concerning bed times and morning rising).
- Be punctual and prepared.
- Look out for any lonely or weaker members of the team, befriend them and assist them.
- Be ready to share the Good News.
- Be culturally, economically and politically sensitive.
- Think before you speak or act – try not to cause offence.

> 'Do not take to heart everything people say, lest you hear your servant cursing you. For many times, also, your own heart has known that even you have cursed others' (Ecclesiastes 7:21-22).

What not to Do

- Do not be selfish or lazy.
- Do not keep the team waiting.
- Do not moan, murmur, criticise or grumble.
- Do not treat your host like a maid or servant.
- Do not hog the shower or use all the hot water – there may be ten people outside queuing for the shower.
- Do not compare your host's: house, car, food, possessions, clothes etc. to yours.
- Do not flaunt your wealth or brag about your money and possessions.
- Do not speak negatively about your host, leader or other team members.
- Do not give your advice on the churches' (or hosts') problems of which you know nothing about, unless the leader, him or herself has asked you.
- Do not demand better food, accommodation or privacy.
- Do not be the group joker, attention seeker or boisterous.

Remember

- You have come to serve.
- Love is a universal language.
- Serve wholeheartedly, joyfully and wear a smile.
- Be flexible, the best of plans often don't work out.
- Beware of cultural faux pas (a socially awkward or tactless act – a slip up).
- Misunderstandings will arise because of differences.
- Laugh at yourself, but be cautious of laughing at others.
- Don't dishonour your team mates, the leader, host or Jesus Christ.
- You may share a room with six people, dozens of insects and some flies! Be kind to humans, but feel free to exterminate the rest, but not in the presence of a Buddhist where all life is sacred.

STM Blessings and Gratitude

- Not being pick pocketed, or having anything stolen, lost or damaged.
- Locals who are happy to help and give directions and local knowledge. Many will go the extra mile.
- Your host and team working together as one.
- Nobody is involved in an accident and the health of the team has been generally good.
- Flying into an airport and getting a visa for free, or for a small amount without any hassle.
- Not having security unpack your rucksack at the airport as a random security check.
- Not having your Gospels, Bibles and tracts etc. taken from you (confiscated in a sensitive nation). Remember that a negative experience can still result in a positive testimony. In some sensitive countries it is unlikely that portions of Scripture, or New Testaments will be destroyed. They may be passed around the police (or army, whoever confiscated them), and will be read out of curiosity. They may even be sold on the black market to people who *really* want them.
- Everything going as planned or better than expected.
- Opportunities to share the Good News, one on one or as part of an evangelistic team.

Chapter 29

Communication and Public Speaking

The apostle Paul wrote to the Church at Corinth, 'And I brethren when I came to you, did not come with excellence of speech or of wisdom declaring to you the testimony of God.... I was with you in weakness, in fear and in much trembling' (1 Corinthians 2:1, 3).

Language difficulties during your short-term mission (STM) combined with unfamiliar social and cultural cues can make communication problematic even on a basic level. Frustration can set in when you are unable to express yourself fully. Learn to laugh at your mistakes and laugh alongside (though not at) the people you are working with and ministering to. When using an interpreter, there may be misunderstandings and miscommunication.

Be clear in your communication, avoid specialised vocabulary, Christian clichés, be aware of your mannerisms and hand gestures. Speak slowly and pause to give the listeners time to think. Make sure your message is culturally relevant when you preach, give your testimony or when sharing the Good News.

It is important that your interpreter *understands* English and the language that he or she is interpreting into! Use plain English; avoid big words, speak slowly, clearly and precisely. Keep sentences short. Avoid slang and phrases or words that are only relevant to your culture. Do not use words which have a double meaning, or of the opposite intended; i.e. wicked – to mean evil or good? Sick – to mean great, vomit/barf or unwell? Keep clear of idioms, colloquialisms, modern sayings or catchphrases, which will only make your interpreter raise his or her arms and give you a blank look.

Preaching, Jokes and Politics via an Interpreter

Respect the time given to you and always give words of greeting before you begin to preach or give your testimony. Remember that preaching through an interpreter will double the length of the sermon and some interpreters will even repeat your message into as many as three or four languages or dialects! Some churches have poor lighting or no natural light and reading from your Bible may be much harder than at home. Get a pair of glasses or a larger print Bible. Jokes rarely bridge cultural divides and can be hard to interpret. Do not preach on politics, democracy or against tyrannical leaders as you could endanger your hosts or cause great offence and harm. Do not discuss these subjects in public places as 'loose talk costs lives,' as the old war saying goes. Poems and songs are also difficult to interpret and rarely if ever make sense to the interpreter or those listening – nonetheless they will still smile and perhaps the interpreter will tell them to clap at the end, to make everyone feel good, but especially you and the team.

If you are part of a team and receive a payment for preaching or giving your testimony, then give it to the leader of the STM for the benefit of the team. Do not see it as your money, but the team's.

Giving your Testimony

Most people going on a STM will not be expected to preach and teach in churches, but in all probability the organization you are with or working alongside will want you to share your testimony, how you became a Christian. Another testimony is what you have learnt since your conversion and how you have progressed in the Christian faith. A thematic testimony focuses on how Jesus Christ has made a difference in your life.

Testimonies are *generally* from 5-10 minutes in length and via an interpreter, will double the length of time. I have walked into churches whilst on STMs as a visitor, unknown to the fellowship and have been asked to come to the front and speak. I will usually talk for 2-3 minutes and give a word of greeting, state who I am, where I am from, the work of my ministry and give a brief word of exhortation to the congregation. After that my mission partner would do the same, but without overlapping our testimonies or work. Do not abuse the opportunity allocated to you. If they want to hear more, they will ask for it or arrange a meeting. Speak slower than your conversational speech; the congregation may not be familiar with your accent.

'For our boasting is this: the testimony of our conscience that we conducted ourselves in the world in simplicity and godly sincerity, not with fleshly wisdom but by the grace of God, and more abundantly towards you' (2 Corinthians 1:12).

Giving a testimony for the first time may be nerve racking, but just explain the basic facts after introducing yourself and give some background information. My name is —. I am from —. The essence of any salvation testimony is: I was a sinner, I repented of my sins, put my faith in Jesus Christ and I trust in Him for my salvation, now and when I die. I am saved by God's grace through faith, not by works, it is God's gift. Remember that nobody is born a Christian, and the importance of any testimony is to put forward truth in a concise and relevant manner. With any testimony beware of giving too much detail that is not relevant. Don't waffle or add unnecessary information. If you are asked to give a testimony then do just that – don't preach or lecture on your favourite theological topic!

A testimony adapts depending on the audience. How you share your testimony to a youth group would be different than if you were speaking to university students, but the message you are trying to get across will always be the same. Stay clear of talking about past girlfriends/boyfriends or if you were divorced etc., as whilst your testimony is your life, it may not go down well in other cultures and could be misunderstood or misinterpreted. Keep it brief and simple. With any testimony, focus on God's grace and mercy rather than focusing on the sins you've committed – do not glory in the devil's former hold over you, avoid sordid details; naming the sin if you so desire is adequate, though unwise in some cultures. Remember to smile, look at the audience (not the floor or the ceiling), scan the room and do not speak too fast. Keep to your allocated time, there may be two or three testimonies after you, and people's attention does wane.

Practise your testimony in front of the mirror and time yourself. When you only practise in front of yourself, it never goes too well, so don't be alarmed or concerned. It will be fine on the day. You may wish to write down some important points on a small prompt card which you can refer to if you get stuck or lost when speaking in public.

'I have not hidden Your righteousness within my heart; I have declared Your faithfulness and Your salvation; I have not concealed Your loving kindness and Your truth from the great congregation' (Psalm 40:10).

Sunday School or Youth Group

You may be asked to speak or share at the Sunday School or youth group so make each talk, testimony or story relevant to your age group. Sunday School talks on the Rich Young Ruler (Luke 18:18-27), the Good Samaritan (Luke 15:11-32), or the Wise and Foolish Builder (Matthew 7:24-27), work well. With any group, remember to raise and lower the tone of your voice and with young children, try to act it out, gesture with your hands and use exaggerated facial expressions. If you are not tied to the pulpit then try and walk around to help act out the story. It makes it exciting for your young audience, perhaps funny in places, but always portray the important truths with seriousness and summarise them at the end with a brief conclusion. Sometimes you can use a Bible story, but put a modern twist to it as long as the same important truth is portrayed – this is why Jesus spoke in parables – contemporary stories that reveal an important message.

'And this I pray, that your love may abound still more and more in knowledge and in all discernment, that you may approve the things that are excellent, that you may be sincere and without offence till the day of Christ, being filled with the fruits of righteousness...' (Philippians 1:9-11).

Selected Passages of Scripture

You may encounter a time when you wish to communicate with other Christians, but your interpreter is not around. One solution is by use of Scripture. If you have a dual language Bible it is much easier, as your first language is on one page and a second language is on the opposite page. Otherwise, you have to turn to your Bible and hope that the other person can turn to it in their Bible. However, even if you cannot read their language you may be able to read the numerals (chapter and verse) and should be able to work out where the Old Testament ends and the New Testament begins. Remember that Psalms is a central marker within the Bible and with 150 chapters cannot easily be missed, and can be used as a reference point for finding other books of the Bible. Look up each Scripture and read it for yourself before you ask the other person to look at it. Make sure that each Scripture is appropriate within the context you are in.

- **Greetings:** 1 Samuel 25:6b, Ephesians 1:2-3, Philippians 1:2, and 1 Timothy 1:2b.
- **General encouragement:** 1 Chronicles 22:16b, 2 Chronicles 15:7, 1 Thessalonians 4:16-18 and 1 Peter 1:3-5.
- **General news and exhortation:** Philippians 3:20, 2 Thessalonians 2:13-17, 2 Thessalonians 3:3-5, 2 Thessalonians 3:13, 2 Thessalonians 3:13 and Hebrews 13:16, 20-22.
- **Why you are there, to share the Good News:** Matthew 9:35-38, Matthew 10:7, Matthew 28:18-20, Mark 16:15-18, Luke 24:46-48, John 4:35, John 20:21 and Acts 1:8.
- **Giving financial aid or gifts for the brethren:** Acts 11:29, Romans 12:13, 2 Corinthians 8:4, 14, 19, 2 Corinthians 9:12, Philippians 4:19 and James 1:27.
- **Persecuted Church, acknowledging them:** Psalm 126:5-6, Proverbs 31:8-9, Hebrews 13:3, 1 Peter 1:6-9 and 1 Peter 3:13-17. (Acknowledging the persecuted Church, can make it easier for those who suffer for their Christian faith).
- **General Church fellowship, the body of Christ:** Matthew 16:15-19, Matthew 18:20, John 13:34-35, John 17:6-26,

Romans 12:4-8, Ephesians 1:22-23, 1 Corinthians 12:4-31 and Hebrews 10:25.

- **General encouragement:** 1 Chronicles 22:16b and 2 Chronicles 15:7.
- **Asking for prayer and encouragement:** Philippians 4:6-7, 1 Thessalonians 3:23-25 and Hebrews 13:8.
- **Praying for you:** Ephesians 1:15-16, Philippians 1:2-6, Colossians 1:2b-6, Colossians 1:9-12 and 2 Thessalonians 1:2-3, 11-12.
- **Goodbyes:** Genesis 31:49, Judges 18:6, 1 Samuel 1:17, Ephesians 6:10, Ephesians 6:23-24, Philippians 4:23, 2 Thessalonians 3:16 and 2 John 3.
- **Hope to return:** 1 Timothy 3:14 and Philippians 2:24.

When Language is Problematic

- Hand gestures often help, you need your room cleaned (pretend to vacuum). You need to drink (cup your hand, bring to your mouth and pour/shake). You need a place to sleep (hands together on their side and put your head on them).
- If you are not sure of the local name for an item, like toilet paper, take a piece with you. Or with your phrase book, point to the relevant item or phrase.
- You can take a clear photo of a destination sign and show it to a taxi or bus driver, or point to it in your guidebook.
- Ask someone who understands you (waiter, receptionist, local missionary) to write out the destination in the local language – especially if the script is different than your own, like Chinese, Korean, Japanese, Russian, Tamil, Urdu, Hebrew or Arabic.
- Take a dual language Bible with you. These have two languages printed on opposite pages making it much easier to communicate with the brethren or when evangelising.
- Dual language Bibles are also an excellent tool when you cannot speak the language yet with prepared selected passages of Scripture, you can still communicate with Christians from the host nation.

In communicating via a second language you need to be understood; not misunderstood, which is a very important point.

Chapter 30

Working with the Locals

The apostle Paul wrote: 'But I know that when I come to you, I shall come in the fullness of the blessing of the Gospel of Christ' (Romans 15:29).

You are going on a short-term mission (STM) to serve others. To serve is also a time to learn – if you're going as a team, working for or alongside a local church or missionary then ask them what help *they* need – not what help *you think* they need! Ask them, "How can we best assist you?" It is vitally important to find out what they want you to do, or what they expect from you. You can email or chat via a webcam or Skype.

A leader may consider flying out several months before the start of a STM (for a week or so) to help oil the cogs of preparation and communication, and to purchase or order the needed materials, working alongside the host. To see what materials or resources are still needed, to confirm any bookings or to inspect the transport, accommodation, (newly laid foundations of a building), to double-check all items and discuss issues with the local host church, ministry or local missionary, so that all parties know what is expected from each other.

There is great difference in logistical planning between a team of eight or eighty STM-ers! Some leaders fly out a week early, ahead of the team to finalise details and to double-check everything. Any tools or materials, which are not available, can then be purchased (weight and size permitting) by the team and flown out with the team.

If you are to construct a home for the pastor, build a church building for the congregation or sink a borehole for the community, find out who is providing the bricks, tools, pumps and all the other related materials and finances. Is planning permission or a permit needed? For a building, make sure the foundations have been laid before the STM team arrives, as they need time to settle and dry.

The host may not have the money to purchase the items needed and if you fly into the country expecting to buy a large quantity of bricks, hundreds of planks of wood or several tons of sand and cement straight from a Western style DIY depot, you may be in for a surprise! The host will more often than not need the money forwarded onto them months in advance so that the materials can be ordered and a deposit paid. The transportation, materials or equipment can take weeks or months to arrive and so forward planning is essential. If you are involved in construction, take into consideration the thoughts, designs, style and workmanship of the locals. Use a local architect, if one is needed – what does your host say? Is planning permission or a permit needed for the new building?

Local families can go hungry when foreigners are willing to do the work for free! Utilise the local expertise and work in partnership. Consider employing members of the church who specialise in certain trades to work alongside you for the two or three weeks of your STM. A days wage for them, say £8 ($12.80) may be an hours wage for you, or half an hour. Your host can inform you of the going rate. The locals may like to begin at dawn, take long lunches or have siestas. Consider all these factors.

Techniques and methods in construction (or evangelism) may also differ; you cannot demand and state, "This is how we do it at home," and proceed to change their set-up, style, method or architecture! How you do a thing at home may not be how it is done on the mission field (for better or for worse).

Priorities, Mutual Respect and Courtesy

In some cultures, relationships and the wider family are more important than tasks – the locals may turn up late, because they stopped to chat to a friend – they are not tied to time. The evangelist meets you an hour later than you had planned, but makes no apology, or the church service cannot 'truly' begin until the pastor arrives and so the morning church service runs into the late afternoon! You may find these situations a great inconvenience (and frustrating), but as you are in their culture, it is you who must give way. Go with the flow and embrace the experience! If the job is not completed, don't see it as a failure because building relationships with the locals is of prime importance.

If you are going to work with a church or group in another area, please treat them with respect and courtesy. Be gracious when inconveniences arise, be forgiving and understanding if the host, pastor congregation or other workers are not punctual, be patient when things are done differently than at home, loving in all situations and void of criticism and murmuring towards all.

Do not embarrass your host, the local church, or your fellow team members by your lack of concern for your brothers and sisters who may have done all in their power to accommodate you and your team, to give you the best of what they have. This is especially true in regards to accommodation and food. Some people will give up their bed for you and sleep on the floor, or move their children into their room so that your small STM team can have some privacy. Would you do that for someone?

Silence is often hard, but golden. You may see an answer to a problem, but you may not have earned the respect to be heard! How would you feel if a stranger came to your church or community and wanted to change things? On the other hand, you may perceive a problem, but to your host or the local church (pastor or individual), there is no problem. You are not on your STM to change the world to your way of thinking, but are there to serve and to emanate and radiate the love of Christ.

If you contact friends at home (or your church or leaders), and things are not as good as you had hoped, then a good rule of thumb is to assume that someone from your host country is reading your email, text message, social media update, letter or fax, or is listening to your phone call! How would they feel if they could read what you have written or listen to your conversation? Do to others, as you would have them do unto you. Do not murmur or speak bad of others.

Remember, as tiredness begins, human grace decreases, so don't stay up late and get out of bed too early. If you are dog-tired you may growl all day! You cannot burn the candle at both ends.

The Freedom of Evangelism
You may live in a fairly free and democratic society where street evangelism is permitted, or where workers openly share the Good News in a variety of formats, door-to-door, literature distribution etc. In some countries, evangelism (to proselytize) is illegal and if a Muslim converts to Christianity (as well as some Hindus, Buddhists or citizens of Communist countries), they will be persecuted or ignored by their family or community, and may even become martyrs for the Christian faith! Therefore, much wisdom is needed in the type and method of evangelism in the place you will be travelling to. Good research and asking your host their advice and opinion *(and what they want done, working in partnership)* will go a long way to make your STM more effective and fruitful for the glory of God. If using tracts or free DVDs, does your host approve of the type you wish to use? These details may appear minor, but are important.

Do not endanger your host, your interpreter or the local missionary who may be undercover. You will go home at the end of your STM, but they have to stay! The missionary could also be expelled from the country. In addition, you do not want to compromise a fellow believer or seeker in a sensitive country, so be wise.

Doctrine and the Local Church
You are in another country to serve people. You may be working alongside a local church for a given period of time, a missionary or assisted by a local evangelist or pastor. You are not there to preach

your denominational doctrine or to harp on about your pet subject; and don't major on the minors. Even Jesus said, "My doctrine is not Mine, but His who sent Me" (John 7:16).

The way you do church and the way your host does church can be very different. You may stand or sit for worship – the opposite of what you do at home; communion/Lord's Supper may be only for those who are adults. You may have to go to the front to receive the bread and wine, (standing up or kneeling) or the servers may come to you. The preacher may expect feedback and the congregation may shout accolades back. Some of the congregation may be dancing in the aisles, hands in the air or clapping, or worshipping without music, others may look as grey as death. Some people may be wearing suits, others could be in shorts and t-shirts.

In many societies, men and women do not sit together in church – even if married. Some do not permit a woman to speak behind the pulpit or to speak in front of men. If you are invited to sit on a raised platform or at the front facing the congregation (both an honour), be careful how you sit – legs crossed can be a no-no and legs apart *is* a no-no. Look around and observe.

Life Changing for the STM-er

As much as going on a STM is about helping others it is also a time for God to reveal to us our character and to help us change ourselves with the opportunities that we encounter. It will also be a time to evaluate our life, our priorities, our worldview and more often than not to see how well-off we actually are compared to the majority of the developing world.

You are not invincible, we do not have all the answers and we, like our host, have failings and difficulties in some areas of our lives. Let us not project an image of what we are not, but be open to learn and to receive help as well as give it when asked to. Remember people's names but especially the host, the leaders, interpreter and evangelist. Some names when heard for the first time can be difficult to pronounce, let alone remember. Ask the person to repeat it and say it out loud. Do this two or three times if need be, to get it lodged in your brain. In many cultures titles are important. If you are introduced to Pastor John, always greet your brother using the title and name, "Pastor John." If the leader does not want to be addressed in such a way, he or she will inform you, or ask them, "How do I address you?"

'Let us not grow weary in doing good...Therefore as we have opportunity, let us do good to all, especially to those who are of the household of faith' (Galatians 6:9-10).

Chapter 31

The Labourer is Worthy of his Wages

'Render therefore to all their due: taxes to whom taxes are due, customs to whom customs are due.... Owe no one anything except to love one another, for he who loves has fulfilled the law.... "You shall love your neighbour as yourself"' (Romans 13:7-9).

A worker is worthy of his hire and those who preach the Gospel should live by the Gospel. If the Western adage is true, 'Time is Money,' then those who have helped you on your short-term mission (STM) should not be overlooked. They should receive remuneration (money or goods for their assistance), but especially Christians, as Scripture declares, '...the labourer is worthy of his wages' (Luke 10:7) and, 'Let us not grow weary in doing good.... Therefore as we have opportunity, let us do good to all, especially to those who are of the household of faith' (Galatians 6:9-10).

The pastor, missionary, evangelist or interpreter who you work with or alongside should all get a fair amount of money for the service they have rendered to the mission team, as well as a love/thank offering, an additional amount of money to bless them and their families. If you are part of a mission organization then these financial issues are not your responsibility, because the mission will take care of it. Do you need to agree on some financial remuneration before your STM begins? The pastor or evangelist may receive a regular wage by the local church, others do not. The interpreter may work freelance (it is his or her profession), therefore what is the fee? Remember, the interpreter still has bills to pay and mouths to feed. Do not take advantage of the generosity of Christians.

Around one billion people (1,000,000,000), more than one in seven people on the planet, survive on less than £1.25 ($2) a day.

If you are hiring a guide, agree a price beforehand, however, some still have a temper tantrum when you pay them! Be polite and just walk away. It is one thing for a local to give you five minutes of their time, but quite another when they go out of their way to take you where you need to go. You may be looking for a specific place or have asked them where the correct bus pick-up point is and it may not be as simple as round the next block. The difficulty can be in trying to evaluate how much you should give a person who has gone out of their way to help you when you have approached them. However, if they have travelled thirty minutes from their home, it is still a thirty-minute return journey and you have encroached upon an hour of their time.

The local pastor, interpreter, evangelist or other Christians may have been an untold blessing to you and the mission team, so how can you repay them? If you ask a Christian, "How much should I give you?" they will more often than not say, "Nothing," "As you like," or ask for a much lesser amount than what you can *actually* give them. What you earn in a week or just a day, may take someone in a developing country a month or more to earn. Your £8 ($12.80) may be one hour's wage, but that may feed the pastor's family for several days. It is always helpful to find out the average income of the country you are going to. How to bless others:

- Pay for all their meals and transport.
- Be a blessing to them and their family.
- Find out their needs, be discreet and sensitive and try to fill them where possible.

Some locals will be hesitant, reluctant or shy to order when you take them to a cafe or food outlet, as to them, the cost may be prohibitive – or just a new experience. Others are used to eating only one or two meals a day. Remind them that you are paying the bill and encourage them to order whatever they want. You may find that on occasions, the local Christians may get over-excited and order too much food. In some countries, individual food items are ordered and everybody around the table (or on the floor) tucks in; there is no *individual* meal. Some out of politeness will order a plain meal, others will order more and take the remainder home for their family. If you are aware of this, then you know at least one way to bless them. You can buy a large bag of rice, maize, potatoes or other staple food, alongside additional items that are not perishable, and give them some money so they can buy (or spend it on) what *they* deem most important. God loves a cheerful giver.

Sometimes the pastor or evangelist does not have the term's fees for their children's education or next month's rent. This is always small in developing countries in comparison to the West. When giving money, state who and what it is for, especially if the money is for personal use, i.e., not for the church funds. Always bless individual workers, but if you have worked with a local church or other ministry, also try and be a blessing to the fellowship or ministry; sometimes you just need to ask, "How can we help?" If giving money to the local church, then inform the pastor that it is for the fellowship, as he or she may think it is for personal use. Some people think it is crass to hand over money – most recipients don't!

Have you ever been a recipient of money or a gift, did you find it crass? You can still buy and pay for items.

- Do they need Bibles, songbooks, chairs or benches?
- Does the church building need renovating? How much would it cost? Ask the pastor if he would like the STM team to employ church members to do the work.

When to Bless Others and Fixers

Experience has taught me that it is best to give a love/thank offering (or an agreed wage) to a person at the end of a mission trip when it is of short duration. But we have always paid for the pastor's, evangelist's or interpreter's transport and expenses (including meals), as and when the need arose. (Some pastors are also the interpreter). If you have an interpreter for several weeks or more, they may prefer payment each week because they have a family who are dependant on them and bills still have to be paid. If you hire a non-Christian interpreter (and occasionally it is the only option and not ideal), then agree on a fee, so that no one feels cheated at the end. Most Christians will interpret within a church setting for free, but this does not mean that they should be overlooked and for some, being an interpreter or a translator is their job (self-employed) and therefore a correct wage should be given to them.

You also need to ask yourself, does the pastor, evangelist, guide or interpreter have enough money to take the bus back to his own home or will he have to walk five miles? At times, a person may prefer to keep the money and walk because the needs of their family are great. Many people live a hand-to-mouth existence (Leviticus 19:13 and Deuteronomy 24:14-15).

'Do not withhold good from those to whom it is due, when it is in the power of your hand to do so. Do not say to your neighbour, "Go, and come back and tomorrow I will give it," when you have it with you' (Proverbs 3:27-28).

Fixers as the name suggest fix things. If you have a problem, they will deal with it or find a solution, whatever the problem. However, if you are working with local Christians they will probably be able to assist. Most fixers receive payment for their help whilst many issues can be solved for free by asking someone on the street! However, top-end fixers intervene with the authorities on your behalf, like when a group needs a visa in a hurry, or a permit, when the consulate is closed or you need a land border crossing to stay open so you can get the team and its minibus through.

Chapter 32

Can you Give Me

'But whoever has this world's goods and sees his brother in need, and shuts up his heart from him; how does the love of God abide in him? My little children let us not love in word or in tongue, but in deed and in truth' (1 John 3:17-18).

In developing countries, poverty is more apparent; more in your face and beggars and/or homeless people can be more numerous and prominent than in the West. Many do not know where their next meal will come from. God has a heart for the poor, for widows, orphans and the fatherless, but how short-term mission (STM) teams respond to appeals from those on the street can be complex. However, there are some Scriptures that can help guide you. Jesus said, "Give to him who asks you..." (Matthew 5:42), but He also stated, "You will always have the poor with you" (Matthew 26:11). You will not solve the problems of world poverty, but you can make a difference in individual's lives, though how and when may be directed by your mission organization or the leader's STM policy.

The policies of STM organizations and local churches concerning 'hand-outs' or gifts vary between each ministry in different countries (even districts and provinces) as no two locations are the same and may vary depending on the circumstances. Whatever rules they have, they have for a good reason and even governments and some local tourist information agencies have their own policies.

Every guidebook to foreign destinations discourages the giving of independent gifts and money, as it encourages a culture of begging; it can cause problems for others and money can be used on substance abuse. They all suggest giving to charities who can distribute to those in need in the most effective manner. However, as a disciple of the Lord Jesus Christ on a STM (not a tourist on holiday/vacation, nor breaking a mission organization's policy), there may be some individuals who through no fault of their own are in dire circumstances, and to pass them by, to ignore their need, would be wrong. See the story of the Good Samaritan (Luke 10:29-37), where the one who did right was not the religious priest or Levite, but the Samaritan, because he had mercy on the man who fell among thieves and was stripped of his possessions. Regardless of where you are in the world, the how, what and when to give, always vexes the most compassionate and kindest of people. There are also professional beggars, con artists and addicts of various types.

You will find these in your home country and abroad. You need to be wise and discerning.

> 'There is one who scatters, yet increases more; and there is one who withholds more than is right, but it leads to poverty. The generous soul will be made rich and he who waters will also be watered himself' (Proverbs 11:24-25).

The Rich Foreigner

Meeting and working with the locals brings new and unexpected challenges to bear and because you are fellow Christians – one in Christ – there are those in developing countries who will ask you for assistance – financially, practically or in other ways. (Many non-Christians may ask as well). There are different ways of looking at this and it varies between cultures. The West has a Protestant work ethic: If you work hard, you will succeed and you will reap the reward of your labour by the sweat of your brow. Whereas others view it differently, "We're brethren; you have, (I need or want), therefore I will ask!" Time and money is part of Western thinking, whereas relationships, friendships and community takes a higher priority in many developing countries. When you return home, you may still receive requests. One man asked for the price of a dowry for a wife!

On your STM, many people you meet will perceive you as the rich foreigner – and compared to them, you probably are. Do not be offended; if you were in their circumstances you would probably do the same. But before you begin to dispense the contents of your wallet or purse, you should speak to your team leader. Always adhere to your mission organization's policy.

Not everybody who asks has a *need*, but a person may *want* some of your perceived wealth, whilst on the other hand, your little gift may go a long way to help a genuine Christian in need.

There is a big difference between your host asking for assistance (or other people who have helped the STM team) and a relative stranger. Many STM teams work with the same church or community and therefore long-term commitments and strong relationships are formed. Visits from a senior leader (of the host church) are often reciprocated whilst the Western church (which is generally financially stronger than those in developing countries), often covers the expenses and will arrange meetings for the leader.

For many STM-ers who have taken a year out, or those not long out of school or college, they will probably not have the disposable income compared to someone who has worked for many years. Therefore, they may not be in a position to help local Christians who ask for financial assistance and that's OK. However, adults should not be asking teenagers for money! One local pastor repeatedly dropped hints about his need, a STM-er responded with respect, "I wish I was rich like you, you're married, have children and have your own home; I cannot afford to get married, start a family or move out and buy my own apartment." No more hints were dropped!

If you lend an item to someone, you can always take a picture of them, so you will not forget who borrowed your item.

How to Handle Requests

So you get asked for money (or items) – what do you do? As a leader you can acknowledge the request or ignore it. There are Christians who work hard and put in long hours for a small wage, and often they have nothing to lose by asking, but everything to gain. Perhaps if we were in their situation we would also do the same. On the other hand, there are some 'Christians' who abuse STM-ers friendship and resort to underhanded tactics to get what they want. Some will play one member of the STM team against another or individually try to solicit money from as many members as they can, or seek out the weaker members of the flock. Some are even so brazen as to pick up items, which belong to STM-ers and walk away with them, or are subtle and admire an object whilst dropping so many hints that it becomes embarrassing. Not everybody who asks is in need – it can be just greed (Proverbs 30:15), however at times, I have appreciated needs being brought to my attention so that I have been able to assist in a more intelligent way.

Whilst we are called to be 'led of the Spirit' (Romans 8:14 and Galatians 5:18a), and not of our emotions, we are to 'walk in the Spirit' (Galatians 5:25), and should make intelligent decisions based on our financial circumstances. It is a sin when we have the power to help someone, but harden our hearts towards them and clench our fists: 'Do not withhold good from those to whom it is due, *when* it is in the power of your hand to do so' (Proverbs 3:27). 'Whoever has this world's goods and sees his brother in need, and shuts up his heart from him, how does the love of God abide in him?' (1 John 3:17). When a 'brother or sister is naked and destitute of daily food and one of you says to them, "Depart in peace, be warmed and filled," but you do not give them the things which are needed for the body, what does it profit?' (James 2:15-16).

Sadly, some STM team's donations, gifts or love offerings which have been given for a specific project or person, have been misappropriated or embezzled by church leaders (or others), and the West is no exception to these sins. Some people will want your money without accountability (and resent it), whereas some are delighted to inform you of the right use of the money. Being accountable is normal in the West, part of routine life, whereas in many developing countries it is seen as a sign of mistrust, "How dare you ask!" If God has told you to give some money, then be obedient and pray that they use it wisely and/or for what it is intended for.

Once I sent a financial gift to a pastor in Sudan and told him that it was for him and his family to spend on their personal needs. Within a few weeks he unexpectedly emailed me with a list of all the things he had spent his money on. This included rent, groceries, school fees and dental work (he had trouble eating at every meal). I did not expect an email, but it was appreciated. On the other hand, a pastor in India (also a head of a Christian ministry) was sent a gift and told to divide it with two other workers who had assisted the team. The lions share was his, 50% with 25% each for the two other workers. It was years later that I found out that he had kept all the money for himself. After emailing, he acknowledged his wrong-doing and was able to trace one of the workers and give him the money.

If you joined a mission organization then all non-verbal requests for assistance should be forwarded onto the mission organization. It may be a situation (or an escalating problem) that needs to be addressed because policies of mutual respect, honesty, trust and cooperation need to be adhered to. It is not right for host churches (whom mission organizations work in partnership with) or individuals from within those churches (even the evangelist or pastor), to try and solicit finances from STM members.

Letter of Invite – Further Education
There may be occasions when a church or a wealthy individual feels called of God to sponsor an individual and each one must be obedient to their heavenly call. On the other hand, there are those who see the potential in an individual and act out of an emotional response, or from a business mind, but neither is being led of the Spirit, and what is the will of the Lord in each individual case? If an anointed preacher or other Christian worker leaves his or her own country to study in another and may never return, it could be a great loss to the home country where perhaps the need is greater. By writing a letter of invite (which is used as part of a visa application process) you may be designating yourself as the financial guarantor of that person whilst he or she is within your country! The person concerned could be your responsibility and you could be liable.

Chapter 33

Expectations and Reality

'I planted, Apollos watered, but God gave the increase. So neither he who plants is anything, nor he who waters, but God who gives the increase. Now he who plants and he who waters are one, and each one will receive his own reward according to his own labour' (1 Corinthians 3:6-8).

You may go on your short-term mission (STM) with great hopes and expectations, but sometimes the reality is different from the preconceived idea or dream. Preaching to crowds of thousands of eager listeners is not the reality of most STMs. Many mission organizations specialise in one-on-one encounters, small meetings, working alongside a local church or participate in humanitarian or development aid as an expression of the love of Christ. I have never known anyone to go on a STM who was not impacted by their time away, whilst many received more than they gave.

In 2000, a senior Christian leader gave advice for those wishing to work in China. 'Come and see how you can serve the vision God has given the Church in China. Together we can seek God about ways to cooperate. You have gifts and resources we don't have, and we have gifts and resources you don't have. Together we can serve the Lord in an effective manner.' Be a servant and serve one another in Christ, see Mark 10:42-45.

Your STM may be just two weeks in duration, so perhaps not as much can be achieved compared with if you stayed for two months. Ask yourself, at home how many people have I witnessed to or led to the Lord within a two-week period? There are many links that make up a chain, and often our witnessing is part of a spiritual chain that leads to a person's conversion. The longer you stay in one destination, the more noticeable the impact that you will have made on individuals, a village or a community. Sometimes, our impact is unbeknown to us and the good influence can be part of a chain of grace that eventually leads someone to Christ.

Some mission fields of the world have good soil and the seed sown, quickly grows and bears fruit as people respond to the Gospel message. Whilst other places are difficult to work in, the ground is hard and stony and the people are unresponsive.

Some STMs can be a case of sowing and planting the seeds of the Good News into people's hearts, whilst another team may see the fruit of the collective labour, as Jesus said, "One sows another reaps," but "both he who sows and he who reaps may rejoice together" (John 4:36-38). The apostle Paul wrote: 'I planted, Apollos watered, but God gave the increase...and each one will receive his own reward according to his labour' (1 Corinthians 3:6, 8).

Most people want to be successful, but what is success? The expectation of a STM differs from one to another. God has not called us to be successful, but faithful and that is our ideal. Our aim is to be in the centre of God's good, perfect and pleasing will and we leave the results up to Him. One sows, another reaps, but we all work towards building His Kingdom. God is glorified when we bear fruit, see John 15:7-8, but fruit has many aspects, and the only place you'll find success before work is in the dictionary!

A missionary once stated, "People ask me, when am I coming home? I answer, when the Lord commands! My duty appears to be to sow the seed of God's Word. I may not reap the harvest, but the sowing is what I am called to. God has rested the reward on my labour for Him and not on success."

Fishers of Men

Jesus was walking by the Sea of Galilee, when he saw two brothers, Simon called Peter, and Andrew. They were casting a net into the sea, for they were fishermen. Jesus said, "Follow Me, and I will make you fishers of men" (Matthew 4:19).

Jesus said, "Go into all the world, and preach the Gospel to every creature" (Mark 16:15). The apostle Paul wrote: 'For whosoever shall call upon the name of the Lord shall be saved. How then shall they call on Him in whom they have not believed? And how shall they believe in Him of whom they have not heard? And how shall they hear without a preacher? And how shall they preach, unless they are sent? As it is written, 'How beautiful are the feet of them that preach the Gospel of peace, and bring glad tidings of good things!' So then faith comes by hearing, and hearing by the Word of God' (Romans 10:13-15, 17).

There is no salvation outside of Jesus Christ, as 'there is no other name under heaven given among men by which we must be saved' (Acts 4:12). Because salvation is a 'must,' we must deliver the message of Jesus Christ and not just the practical mercy of Christ's love. We must proclaim the Good News in an intelligent and relevant manner, Jesus' life, death and resurrection because 'whoever calls upon the name of the Lord will be saved' (Romans 10:13), and they must repent, accept the free gift of eternal life and live for Him. They will become 'born again' (John 3:3, 7), passing from 'death to life' (John 5:24 and 1 John 3:14), and will receive forgiveness of sins; being washed (spiritually speaking) by the shed blood of Jesus

Christ because of their faith in His atoning work. The apostle Paul became all things to all men to save some (1 Corinthians 9:19-22). As we are called to be fishers of men then like fishermen, we need to use different types of bait (methods or approaches) to catch different types of fish.

We must remember that when we try to catch fish, by sharing the Good News, that people will be dirty and will need a lot of cleaning up, training and discipleship. Sadly, many churches expect the fish to be clean before they can be caught, but this is not what Jesus taught, saying, "Those who are well have no need of a physician, but those who are sick. I did not come to call the righteous, but sinners to repentance" (Mark 2:17).

Whilst we should be realistic on our STM, we do serve the God of the impossible, and who knows what might happen in expectant faith. The prophet Jonah was most reluctant to preach to the Assyrians in Nineveh, and tried to run from the call of God. But when he preached to the unevangelised city of Nineveh declaring the Word of the Lord, "Yet forty days and Nineveh shall be overthrown!" The people believed the Word as from God, repented and turned from their evil ways! (Jonah chapter 3).

'Ask of Me, and I will give You the nations for Your inheritance, and the ends of the earth for Your possession' (Psalm 2:8).

Inspiring Mission Related Scriptures
- 'Declare His glory among the nations, His wonders among all peoples' (Psalm 96:3).
- 'Arise, O God, judge the earth; for You shall inherit all nations' (Psalm 82:8).
- 'I will go in the strength of the Lord God; I will make mention of Your righteousness, of Yours only' (Psalm 71:16).
- 'That men may know that You, whose name alone is the Lord, are the Most High over all the earth' (Psalm 83:18).
- '...The people who know their God shall be strong and carry out great exploits' (Daniel 11:32b).
- '...Be steadfast, immovable...your labour in the Lord is not in vain' (1 Corinthians 15:58).
- "I have come to do Your will O God" (Hebrews 10:9).

Chapter 34

Preparing to Return Home

'He has taken a bag...with him and will come home on the appointed day' (Proverbs 7:20).

At the end of the short-term mission (STM), either in your host country or when you arrive back at home, there should be a debriefing meeting which should consist of every member of the team. It is an opportunity to try to adjust to some level of normality as you try to fit back into your home settings, and a time where you talk and discuss the STM. Each member of the team should have an opportunity to share their thoughts, highlights, (and their lows), experiences and what they have learnt. The team, not the leader, should do the majority of the talking. The leader acts more as a chairperson and guides the group. If possible, there should be an anonymous questionnaire to fill out where each member can comment and rate the STM and generally evaluate the trip from their perspective. This could be in the form of questions with ratings e.g. from 1-5: very good (1), good (2), not sure (3), ok (4), bad (5). Or: excellent, good, ok, adequate, poor. Questions can be about: the food, travel, accommodation, the work you did, the locals you worked with, the working hours, rest and relaxation, the rules and structure of the STM, the leader, translator etc. There also needs to be space for comments, suggestions and improvements. This will aid the leader or mission organization with planning and implementing future STMs.

Jesus sent out the seventy on their STMs and when they came back, they reported to Him all that had happened (Luke 10:1, 17-20).

Before you Depart for Home

You may have some items of clothing or other possessions that you brought to the mission field which would be far better used or appreciated by the locals. If you are with a mission organization speak to your leader before you give items or money away – seek their advice as what to do. Problems arise when someone receives a gift and somebody else does not. It can cause friction and tension. There is also a danger that individuals will be friendly to future STM-er because of what they can get out of it and can lead to a culture of begging. You could give your excess items to someone you work alongside (a local) or a person you ministered to, a new friend or someone who looks in need. You may wish to leave some money behind, instead of converting your spare cash back into your own currency (but leave some money for the airport!) or use this money to buy present(s) – something which an individual or a church needs. You may be in a position to hand over some of your own currency. £10 ($16) may *just* be a monthly phone top up for someone in the West, but it is eight days living expenses for those who live on £1.25 ($2) a day!

Sometimes money is given to the church you have worked with (or the local missionary who has arranged things for you) and in this way, it can be better utilised. If STM teams frequently work with the church, it can cause problems when one team gives x amount and another team gives less.

Before you leave your STM, there are things you should do and other things which you may like to do. You should thank the team leader, interpreter, pastor, evangelist, guide, the cooks, the host church and whoever else has helped you. (The team may write a thank you card, signed by all participants, but not in sensitive nations). Say your goodbyes to the rest of the team (if you are not flying back together), get their email addresses or social media contacts if you intend to keep in touch. Be sensible to whom you give your contact details to outside of the team. You may exchange emails and never hear from the person again. The pastor or host may not have the time to keep in contact with everyone.

You will probably be asked for your home address; email and telephone number by many people, though there is a difference between the people that you have worked alongside for days or weeks and the stranger you talked to for twenty minutes on the street. Remember, international phone calls can be expensive and your friend may phone you and ask you to ring back! If you cannot afford to, then tell them.

The leader of a STM team should confirm the flight details three days or thereabouts before departure. The day before departure, settle all the bills (accommodation, gifts and other expenses), and confirm that the team has transport to the airport. Pack your bag. If you have stayed with a host or at a mission compound, tidy up! Check-in online 24hrs before departure and you get to choose your seat on the flight home. On the day of departure, check the rooms and leave in plenty of time, as it is better to wait around for three hours at the airport than to miss the flight because the vehicle broke down or because the train was delayed. Keep your plane ticket, passport and any valuables on you!

Your hand/carry-on luggage must be accessible at all times. If you need to phone home on arrival via a public call box. Carry some change in your pocket or in your hand/carry-on luggage.

Promises and Emotional Bonds

In the Western world there is an underlying culture of misleading politeness, which entails not telling the truth. A common form is making promises and not fulfilling them, "I'll keep in touch," and you never: write, email, phone or add them as a friend on social media! "I'll send you the book, photo, clothes, CD, DVD" etc. and you don't. It is a culture that has developed out of politeness and good intentions, but in different countries is taken as a promise; not just a loose saying. In the heat of the moment, the emotion of the mission or whilst saying our goodbyes we are prone to say the most normal, yet bizarre statements – "You must come and visit me sometime," – "If you're in — look me up." Even after the STM has ended it has been known for the host or a member of the church to phone the STM-er from the airport or even turn up on the STM-ers doorstep unannounced, with no place to stay, little money and a three month tourist visa!

Do not make a promise that you cannot keep or have no intention of keeping. The reply, "I'll think about it," in response to a request, can also be interpreted in other cultures as "yes," or that you will get back to them, whereas in the West it is often used as polite way to get someone to stop pestering you.

Do not be foolish like some STM-ers who have offered designer trainer/sneakers, scholarships, visas, plane tickets, money for schooling/buildings, trips to theme parks, mobile/cell phones, books, CDs, DVDs, letters of recommendation/invites and even a promise to return next year. Broken promises can shatter dreams and hopes. Breaking your word tarnishes your reputation, that of the mission organization, or your church, shows little regard to the one you have promised and dishonours the name of the Lord.

Write any promises or obligations down (type them into your smartphone) and if you are unable to fulfill them, then let the person know, and give a good valid reason wrapped in love and sympathy for your backtracking. Sometimes we do forget things, it happens. At other times, international postage/shipping can be prohibitive.

Working with the locals can produce emotional bonds, ties of friendship which can last for years or even decades and can be emotionally traumatic when you have to part. Don't be ashamed of crying, you may have mixed emotions, sad to leave but happy to go. If your host comes and visits your country try to be as helpful towards them as they were to you, or better!

You may feel sorry for those you leave behind (and that is not a bad thing), but they also may feel sorry for you, going back to the rat-race of a Western materialistic society.

Chapter 35

Back at Home

When Paul and Barnabas completed their first missionary trip, they returned to their church at 'Antioch where they had been commended to the grace of God for the work they had completed. And when they had come and gathered the church together, they reported all that God had done with them and that He had opened the door of faith to the Gentiles' (Acts 14:26-27).

Your short-term mission (STM) may end when you arrive back at home and you could be greeted with all sorts of emotions, from jubilation to depression, loneliness, disorientation or reverse culture shock; and there will be many things that need to be done. There will be your bag to unpack, clothes to wash, friends and family wanting to know how the STM went, or for the undiscerning churchgoer, "How was your holiday/vacation?" There will be a small mountain of correspondence to deal with, bank statements to check, junk mail to wade through and a whole host of other things.

Arriving back at 'home' can be daunting, especially the affluence, excess and waste of resources – this is most noticeable when you return from a developing country. You can feel ashamed at yourself for having a wardrobe/closet full of clothes, numerous pairs of shoes, the latest gadgets and three meals a day, whereas the people you were working alongside or ministering to may have been less fortunate than yourself, some of whom may have lived a day-to-day existence. Do not make any rash decisions like throwing the contents of your wardrobe/closet away, but prayerfully ask yourself, "What can I learn from this?" Perhaps, instead of buying all the latest clothes, music, DVDs and accumulating so many items in the future, the money could be better utilised to help those whom you left behind, to assist others to go on STMs or pay for Bibles to those who cannot afford them.

Things to Do on Your Return

The following list is a general guide of things to do, largely dependent on what time of day or night you get back, and your own particular routine.

1. Give thanks to the Lord (and whilst on the STM also).
2. Unpack your bag and put the washing machine on.

3. Have a hot shower or bath. You may really need it, or you will certainly appreciate it after your long journey home.
4. Have a powernap or sleep, especially if you have had a night flight, or you may just be generally tired.
5. Put washing out to dry or ask someone to do it for you.
6. Open your correspondence and throw away the junk mail. Leave checking your bank statements for another time when you are fresh.
7. Check your emails and social media.
8. Sort your digital photos out and save them.

Within a Few Days you Will Need to
1. Let your friends, family, supporters and church know that you are home (just in case they don't know). Phone, email, SMS, or via social media, though some elderly people appreciate a phone call or a letter, especially if they are not a silver surfer (they are retired and do not use the internet).
2. Write a summary or report of the mission – if not for yourself, for those who have prayed or financially supported you. Go through your journal for highlights and/or look through your sent emails whilst you were on your STM and use that as a framework. Your church may want you to give your testimony of your STM, or you may want to tell them (and you should) – go see your pastor or youth leader. You may be able to use your report for the church newsletter, but do not include any sensitive information.
3. Fulfill your obligations and discharge your duties, by sending photos, CDs, DVDs or books etc. to those you have promised. These items do not always arrive and don't expect an acknowledgment of thanks. Email them and let them know you have posted/shipped the items, even if the items never arrive, they know you have fulfilled your word. Sending Bibles (and items of value) to sensitive countries is hit and miss.
4. Write letters, send emails or a friend request, to those whom you said you would keep in contact with. Send thank you emails, letters or social media updates to those who helped you, and don't forget your host (if you worked with a local church). However, be cautious of what you write if you worked in a sensitive country.
5. Get a job or continue with your studies, but try to have a few days rest on your return before resuming a routine. You may still be jetlagged or may even be unwell for a few days.
6. If you think you may have caught something, see a doctor and tell them where you have come back from. Malaria and

other diseases or infections can appear months after your return, even up to two years!

Other Helpful Things

Add up the total cost of your STM. This is easier if you joined a mission organization as you only have a few items to add. However, working out the cost of your mission and dividing it by the number of days you were there is an interesting sum and helps you budget for future missions. By now, you would have probably have written a report of your trip (for the church newsletter and your supporters), but for your own record, evaluate the STM and make a note of several factors:

- What you learnt.
- What God taught you.
- How could I have been more effective?
- What things would I have done differently?
- Things to remember for the next time (what items would have been great to take and what to leave at home) etc.
- The total cost of the STM.

Jesus said, "In as much as you did it to one of the least of these My brethren you did it to Me" (Matthew 25:35-46).

Freedom and Caution

The West has huge amounts of freedom which has arisen from our Christian heritage and our forefathers who fought for those rights. See *How Christianity Made the Modern World* by Paul Backholer. In other parts of the world, these "rights" do not exist. You have to be wise whilst on your STM, but just as wise on your return. Be careful what you publish, email, write in a newsletter/social media, or allow to be put into print, especially if you have worked in a Muslim, Buddhist or Communist town, district or country. It can cause problems for the locals, new converts, the local church or highlights the authorities that stricter controls are needed in the future. Being too open can hinder future mission work in some districts or countries.

The Next Step

Your STM would have been a life changing experience at best, but on the lower end of the scale you would still have learnt many things (about yourself and others). Where you go from now is between you and the Lord. You may have got a taste for STMs and hunger for more or feel that they are not for you, but you still want to see the fulfilment of the Great Commission (Matthew 28:19-20 and Mark 16:15-18). Why not be the missionary in your work place, college or university? Also, as much as your disposable income dictates, assist others to go on a STM and take your place by proxy! For others, their STM may be a stepping-stone or a turning point that will eventually lead them to become a full-time missionary or other Christian worker. For some, they will be infused to become a mission mobiliser, one who mobilises and encourages others to go on missions. They help raise support and awareness for missions, both prayerfully and financially.

Jesus said, "He who is faithful in what is least is faithful also in much; and he who is unjust in what is least is unjust also in much. Therefore if you have not been faithful in the unrighteous mammon, who will commit to your trust the true riches? And if you have not been faithful in what is another man's, who will give you what is your own?" (Luke 16:10-12).

Remember To
- Continue to pray for the mission organization or local church that you worked with, as well as those you met, helped and ministered to.
- Keep in touch with other members of your team.
- Encourage others to go on STMs.
- Perhaps you are already planning on going on another STM next year!
- If you are able to, I would encourage you to give more of your disposable income towards the fulfilment of the Great Commission: support mission organizations, missionaries and Bible translation/printing etc. Perhaps your church could support others to go on a STM?
- A small monthly amount (e.g. £10+/$16+) can help support indigenous Christian workers, such as an evangelist.
- If this book has blessed you, then why not bless others with a copy (also available as an eBook), give a shout-out on social media and write a short (or long) review on your favourite review site. Thank you. ☺

www.MissionsNow.co.uk

Free online Discipleship Course: www.byfaith.co.uk/paulni5.htm.

Other Books by Mathew Backholer

Christian Missions
- How to Plan, Prepare and Successfully Complete Your Short-Term Mission: For Churches, Independent STM Teams and Mission Organizations.
- Short-Term Missions, A Christian Guide to STMs: For Leaders, Pastors, Churches, Students, STM Teams and Mission Organizations – Survive and Thrive!

World Travel
- Budget Travel, a Guide to Travelling on a Shoestring, Explore the World, a Discount Overseas Adventure Trip.

Christian Discipleship and Spiritual Growth
- Extreme Faith, On Fire Christianity: Hearing from God and Moving in His Grace, Strength & Power – Living in Victory.
- Discipleship For Everyday Living, Christian Growth: Following Jesus Christ and Making Disciples of All Nations.

Christian Revivals and Awakenings
- Revival Fires and Awakenings, Thirty-Six Visitations of the Holy Spirit: A Call to Holiness, Prayer and Intercession for the Nations.
- Global Revival, Worldwide Outpourings, Forty-Three Visitations of the Holy Spirit: The Great Commission.
- Revival Answers, True and False Revivals: Genuine or Counterfeit? Do not be Deceived, Discerning between the Holy Spirit and the Demonic.
- Revival Fire, 150 Years of Revivals: Spiritual Awakenings and Moves of the Holy Spirit.
- Understanding Revival and Addressing the Issues it Provokes.
- Reformation to Revival, 500 Years of God's Glory: Sixty Revivals, Awakenings and Heaven-Sent Visitations of the Holy Spirit.

www.ByFaithBooks.co.uk

Social Media
www.facebook.com/ByFaithMedia
www.instagram.com/ByFaithMedia
www.youtube.com/ByFaithMedia
www.twitter.com/ByFaithMedia

Sources and Notes

Chapter 2
1. See also Luke 24:47, John 4:35 and John 20:21-23.
2. Advice on Money management: www.byfaith.co.uk/paulmoney.html. In *Discipleship For Everyday Living: Christian Growth* by Mathew Backholer, ByFaith Media, 2011, there are three chapters on finances and Christian workers.

Chapter 3
1. *An Instrument of Revival – The Complete Life of Evan Roberts 1878-1951* by Brynmor Pierce Jones, Bridge Publishing, 1995, page 205.

Chapter 4
1. *Hudson Taylor and the China Inland Mission – The Growth of a Work of God* by Dr. and Mrs. Howard Taylor, China Inland Mission, 1918, 1940, page 355.
2. *Hudson Taylor in Early Years – The Growth of a Soul* by Dr. and Mrs Howard Taylor, China Inland Mission, 1911, 1940, pages 372-373.

Chapter 8
1. *Discipleship For Everyday Living: Christian Growth* by Mathew Backholer, ByFaith Media, 2011, page 44.

Chapter 23
1. Asia Harvest Newsletter #109, May 2011, page 6.

Chapter 25
1. *Power Evangelism – Revised and Updated with Study Guide* by John Wimber with Kevin Springer, Hodder and Stoughton, 1985, 1992, page 129.
2. *Failure Is Never Final* by Lynda Neilands, Christian Focus, 1994, 2000, page 114.

Chapter 26
1. *Candidates in Waiting* by Georgina A. Gollock, CMS, 1892, 1898, page 74.

Chapter 27
1. See *Extreme Faith, On Fire Christianity* by Mathew Backholer, ByFaith Media, for additional Scriptural declarations and biblical explanations.

Chapter 28
1. *Ascent of the Inner Everest* by Leonard Moules, Christian Literature Crusade, 1971, pages 26 and 30.

www.ByFaith.co.uk

www.MissionsNow.co.uk

www.RevivalNow.co.uk

ByFaith Media Books

The following ByFaith Media books are available as paperback and eBooks, whilst some are also available as hardbacks.

Short-Term Missions (Christian Travel with a Purpose)
How to Plan, Prepare and Successfully Complete Your Short-Term Mission by Mathew Backholer. *For Churches, Independent STM Teams and Mission Organizations.* This book will guide you through all you need to know about STMs and includes: mission statistics, cultural issues, where and when to go, what to do, food and accommodation, quotes, Bible verses and more than 140 real-life STM testimonies.

Short-Term Missions, A Christian Guide to STMs by Mathew Backholer. *For Leaders, Pastors, Churches, Students, STM Teams and Mission Organizations – Survive and Thrive!* What you need to know about planning a STM, or joining a STM team, and considering the options as part of the Great Commission.

Christian Discipleship
Discipleship For Everyday Living, Christian Growth: Following Jesus Christ and Making Disciples of All Nations by Mathew Backholer. Engaging biblical teaching to aid believers in maturity, to help make strong disciples with solid biblical foundations who reflect the image of Jesus Christ.

Extreme Faith, On Fire Christianity: Hearing from God and Moving in His Grace, Strength & Power – Living in Victory by Mathew Backholer. Discover the powerful biblical foundations for on fire faith in Christ! God has given us powerful weapons to defeat the enemy, to take back the spiritual land in our lives and to walk in His glory through the power of the Holy Spirit.

Budget Travel – Holiday/Vacations
Budget Travel, a Guide to Travelling on a Shoestring, Explore the World, a Discount Overseas Adventure Trip: Gap Year, Backpacking, Volunteer-Vacation and Overlander by Mathew Backholer. A practical and concise guide to travelling the world and exploring new destinations with fascinating opportunities and experiences.

Revivals and Spiritual Awakenings
Global Revival, Worldwide Outpourings, Forty-Three Visitations of the Holy Spirit: The Great Commission by Mathew Backholer. With forty-three revivals from more than thirty countries on six continents, the author reveals the fascinating links between pioneering missionaries

and the revivals that they saw as they worked towards the Great Commission.

Revival Fires and Awakenings, Thirty-Six Visitations of the Holy Spirit: A Call to Holiness, Prayer and Intercession for the Nations by Mathew Backholer. With 36 fascinating accounts of revivals in nineteen countries from six continents, plus biblical teaching on revival, prayer and intercession. Also available as a hardback.

Revival Fire, 150 Years of Revivals, Spiritual Awakenings and Moves of the Holy Spirit by Mathew Backholer, documents in detail, twelve revivals from ten countries on five continents. Through the use of detailed research, eye-witness accounts and interviews, *Revival Fire* presents some of the most potent revivals that the world has seen in the past one hundred and fifty years.

Revival Answers, True and False Revivals, Genuine or Counterfeit Do not be Deceived by Mathew Backholer. What is genuine revival and how can we tell the true from the spurious? Drawing from Scripture with examples across Church history, this book will sharpen your senses and take you on a journey of discovery.

Reformation to Revival, 500 Years of God's Glory by Mathew Backholer. For the past five hundred years God has been pouring out His Spirit, to reform and to revive His Church. *Reformation to Revival* traces the Divine thread of God's power from Martin Luther of 1517, through to the Charismatic Movement and into the twenty-first century, featuring sixty great revivals from twenty nations.

Understanding Revival and Addressing the Issues it Provokes by Mathew Backholer. Many who have prayed for revival have rejected it when it came because they misunderstood the workings of the Holy Spirit and only wanted God to bless the Church on their terms. Learn to intelligently cooperate with the Holy Spirit during times of revivals and Heaven-sent spiritual awakenings.

Christian Teaching and Inspirational
Tares and Weeds in Your Church: Trouble & Deception in God's House, the End Time Overcomers by R. B. Watchman. Is there a battle taking place in your house, church or ministry, leading to division? Tares and weeds are counterfeit Christians used to sabotage Kingdom work; learn how to recognise them and neutralise them in the power of the Holy Spirit.

Holy Spirit Power: Knowing the Voice, Guidance and Person of the Holy Spirit by Paul Backholer. Power for Christian living; drawing from the powerful influences of many Christian leaders, including: Rees Howells,

Evan Roberts, D. L. Moody, Duncan Campbell and other channels of God's Divine fire.

Jesus Today, Daily Devotional: 100 Days with Jesus Christ by Paul Backholer. Two minutes a day to encourage and inspire; 100 days of daily Christian Bible inspiration to draw you closer to God. *Jesus Today* is a concise daily devotional defined by the teaching of Jesus and how His life can change yours.

Samuel Rees Howells: A Life of Intercession by Richard Maton is an in-depth look at the intercessions of Samuel Rees Howells alongside the faith principles that he learnt from his father, Rees Howells, and under the guidance of the Holy Spirit. With 39 black and white photos in the paperback and hardback editions.

The Baptism of Fire, Personal Revival, Renewal and the Anointing for Supernatural Living by Paul Backholer. The author unveils the life and ministry of the Holy Spirit, shows how He can transform your life and what supernatural living in Christ means. Filled with biblical references, testimonies from heroes of the faith and the experiences of everyday Christians, you will learn that the baptism of fire is real and how you can receive it!

Supernatural and Spiritual
Glimpses of Glory, Revelations in the Realms of God Beyond the Veil in the Heavenly Abode: The New Jerusalem and the Eternal Kingdom of God by Paul Backholer. In this narrative receive biblical glimpses and revelations into life in paradise, which is filled with references to Scripture to confirm its veracity. A gripping read!

Prophecy Now, Prophetic Words and Divine Revelations for You, the Church and the Nations by Michael Backholer. An enlightening end-time prophetic journal of visions, words and prophecies.

Heaven, A Journey to Paradise and the Heavenly City by Paul Backholer. Join one person's exploration of paradise, guided by an angel and a glorified man, to witness the thrilling promise of eternity, and to provide answers to many questions about Heaven. Anchored in the Word of God, discover what Heaven will be like!

Biography and Autobiography
Samuel, Son and Successor of Rees Howells: Director of the Bible College of Wales – A Biography by Richard Maton. The author invites us on a lifelong journey with Samuel, to unveil his ministry at the College and the support he received from numerous staff, students and visitors, as the history of BCW unfolds alongside the Vision to reach Every Creature with the Gospel. With 113 black and white photos in the paperback and hardback editions!

The Holy Spirit in a Man: Spiritual Warfare, Intercession, Faith, Healings and Miracles by R. B. Watchman. One man's compelling journey of faith and intercession – a gripping true-life story. Raised in a dysfunctional family and called for a Divine purpose. Sent out by God, he left employment to claim the ground for Christ, witnessing signs and wonders, spiritual warfare and deliverance.

Historical and Adventure

Britain, A Christian Country, A Nation Defined by Christianity and the Bible & the Social Changes that Challenge this Biblical Heritage by Paul Backholer. For more than 1,000 years Britain was defined by Christianity, discover this continuing legacy, how faith defined its nationhood and the challenges from the 1960s onwards.

How Christianity Made the Modern World by Paul Backholer. Christianity is the greatest reforming force that the world has ever known, yet its legacy is seldom comprehended. See how Christianity helped create the path that led to Western liberty and laid the foundations of the modern world.

Celtic Christianity & the First Christian Kings in Britain: From St. Patrick and St. Columba, to King Ethelbert and King Alfred by Paul Backholer. Celtic Christians ignited a Celtic Golden Age of faith and light which spread into Europe. Discover this striking history and what we can learn from the heroes of Celtic Christianity.

Lost Treasures of the Bible: Exploration and Pictorial Travel Adventure of Biblical Archaeology by Paul Backholer. Join a photographic quest in search of the lost treasures of the Bible. Unveil ancient mysteries as you discover the evidence for Israel's exodus from Egypt, and travel into lost civilisations in search of the Ark of the Covenant. Explore lost worlds with over 160 colour pictures and photos in the paperback edition.

The Exodus Evidence In Pictures – The Bible's Exodus: The Hunt for Ancient Israel in Egypt, the Red Sea, the Exodus Route and Mount Sinai by Paul Backholer. Brothers, Paul and Mathew Backholer search for archaeological data to validate the biblical account of Joseph, Moses and the Hebrew Exodus from ancient Egypt. With more than 100 full colour photographs and graphics in the paperback edition.

The Ark of the Covenant – Investigating the Ten Leading Claims by Paul Backholer. The mystery of the Bible's lost Ark of the Covenant has led to many myths, theories and claims. Join two explorers as they investigate the ten major theories concerning the location of antiquities greatest relic. 80+ colour photographs in the paperback edition.

ByFaith Media DVDs

Christian Travel (Backpacking Style Short-Term Mission)

ByFaith – World Mission on 1 DVD is a Christian reality TV show that reveals the real experience of a backpacking style short-term mission in Asia, Europe and North Africa. Two brothers, Paul and Mathew Backholer shoot through fourteen nations, in an 85-minute real-life documentary. Filmed over three years, *ByFaith – World Mission* is the very best of ByFaith TV season one.

Revivals and Spiritual Awakenings

Great Christian Revivals on 1 DVD is an inspirational and uplifting account of some of the greatest revivals in Church history. Filmed on location across Britain and drawing upon archive information, the stories of the Welsh Revival (1904-1905), the Hebridean Revival (1949-1952) and the Evangelical Revival (1739-1791) are brought to life in this moving 72-minute documentary. Using computer animation, historic photos and depictions, the events of the past are weaved into the present, to bring these Heaven-sent revivals to life.

Historical and Adventure

Israel in Egypt – The Exodus Mystery on 1 DVD. A four year quest searching for Joseph, Moses and the Hebrew slaves in Egypt. Join Paul and Mathew Backholer as they hunt through ancient relics and explore the mystery of the biblical exodus, hunt for the Red Sea and climb Mount Sinai. Discover the first reference to Israel outside of the Bible, uncover depictions of people with multicoloured coats, encounter the Egyptian records of slaves making bricks and find lost cities. 110 minutes. The very best of *ByFaith – In Search of the Exodus*.

ByFaith – Quest for the Ark of the Covenant on 1 DVD. Join two adventurers on their quest for the Ark, beginning at Mount Sinai where it was made, to Pharaoh Tutankhamun's tomb, where Egyptian treasures evoke the majesty of the Ark. The quest proceeds onto the trail of Pharaoh Shishak, who raided Jerusalem. The mission continues up the River Nile to find a lost temple, with clues to a mysterious civilization. Crossing through the Sahara Desert, the investigators enter the underground rock churches of Ethiopia, find a forgotten civilization and examine the enigma of the final resting place of the Ark itself. 100+ minutes.

www.ingramcontent.com/pod-product-compliance
Lightning Source LLC
LaVergne TN
LVHW051125080426
835510LV00018B/2241